Few things are as challenging or rewarding a[nd trust] me, you'll take all the help you can get. This [book will chal]lenge you, and inspire you.

MARK BATTERSON, *New York Times* bestselling author of
The Circle Maker, lead pastor of National Community Church

Full of refreshing perspective and practical help for every parent, *Raising Amazing* will give you a vision for the family you long for.

RUTH CHOU SIMONS, mom to six boys, *Wall Street Journal*
bestselling author, and founder of gracelaced.com

We all need guides, especially in parenting, and Monica is an incredible guide to raising a family that loves each other *because they love God first.* This book deserves the name—it's a truly *amazing* resource for parents who want to follow Jesus as they raise their kids.

JUSTIN WHITMEL EARLEY, lawyer, speaker, and
author of *Habits of the Household*

Monica Swanson walks her talk—and her kids are walking, talking testimonies that these parenting principles work! If what you've been doing isn't working, *Raising Amazing* offers biblical help that you can put into practice immediately. Monica's inspiring wisdom and actionable takeaways will equip you with everything you need to raise an amazing family who loves God and each other. *Raising Amazing* is . . . well . . . amazing!

WENDY SPEAKE, coauthor of *Triggers: Exchanging Parents' Angry Reactions for Gentle Biblical Responses,* host of The 40-Day Sugar Fast

Today's kids are shaped by a thousand voices and influences—and for parents, this means *our* voice and *our* influence has gained unprecedented importance. Rather than shy away from this call, it's time to step up, and through Monica Swanson, you have a wise and winsome friend to propel that journey.

KARI KAMPAKIS, bestselling author of *Love Her Well* and
More Than a Mom, host of the *Girl Mom* podcast

Raising Amazing is one of the best parenting books I've read. It's Jesus-centric, fun, and *uber*practical. One of this book's dozens of practices can change your life. But Monica makes it easy to adopt *many* of them!

JORDAN RAYNOR, bestselling author of *The Creator in You* and *Redeeming Your Time*

Rarely do I encounter a parenting book that is both inspirational and practical. This is it! Monica is the "mentor mom" we're all looking for, and she has generously shared her insights with us on these pages. Her wisdom springs from her personal experience as a mom of four boys, current research, and most of all, her deep and long-standing friendship with Jesus. I am grateful for Monica's gracious and countercultural voice, and I know you will be too!

NICOLE ZASOWSKI, licensed marriage and family therapist, author of *What If It's Wonderful?*

Raising Amazing is the best book for practical godly wisdom on how to raise children the way God wants us to. Monica nailed it! I cheered in my heart while reading the book from cover to cover and cried when I finished it. A mandatory must-read if you have children!

RACHEL-RUTH LOTZ WRIGHT, coauthor of *Jesus Followers*

Raising Amazing might feel like an intimidating title. Maybe you feel like you are *barely raising*, let alone *raising amazing*. Trust me, as a mom of five boys who range from six to twenty-six, I get it. But here's the good news: Monica doesn't define "amazing" as something you must produce in your kids. Rather, "amazing" is all about parenting on a foundation of God's amazing grace. Our children's choices are between them and the Lord, but Monica shows us how we can partner with the Holy Spirit to plant seeds that, God willing, will produce amazing fruit.

JEANNIE CUNNION, author of *Mom Set Free* and *Don't Miss Out*

Just reading the title makes this mama of seven raise her hand and say, "Sign me up for that!" Monica's gracious way of explaining God's truth for our families without pushing a formula for having perfect kids is refreshing, honest, and real. This book is a great reminder of my role as a parent and God's role as the ruler of all things . . . and thank the Lord for that!

KIRSTEN WATSON, author of *Sis, Take a Breath*,
executive editor of MomLife Today

RAISING Amazing

Bringing Up Kids Who Love God, Like Their Family, and Do the Dishes

WITHOUT BEING ASKED

MONICA SWANSON

ZONDERVAN
BOOKS

ZONDERVAN BOOKS

Raising Amazing
Copyright © 2023 by Monica Swanson

Requests for information should be addressed to:
Zondervan, *3900 Sparks Dr. SE, Grand Rapids, Michigan 49546*

Zondervan titles may be purchased in bulk for educational, business, fundraising, or sales promotional use. For information, please email SpecialMarkets@Zondervan.com.

ISBN 978-0-310-36528-0 (audio)

Library of Congress Cataloging-in-Publication Data

Names: Swanson, Monica, author.
Title: Raising amazing : bringing up kids who love God, like their family, and do the dishes without being asked / Monica Swanson.
Description: Grand Rapids : Zondervan, 2023. | Summary: "As a mom of four boys, author and podcast host Monica Swanson knows firsthand the challenges of parenting. Raising Amazing combines years of research and many of her own personal stories to equip you to raise amazing kids of godly character and deep faith who love and honor their parents and remain close to their siblings for a lifetime"—Provided by publisher.
Identifiers: LCCN 2022034711 (print) | LCCN 2022034712 (ebook) | ISBN 9780310365266 (trade paperback) | ISBN 9780310365273 (ebook)
Subjects: LCSH: Families—Religious life. | Families—Religious aspects—Christianity. | Parenting—Religious aspects—Christianity. | Interpersonal relations—Religious aspects—Christianity. | BISAC: RELIGION / Christian Living / Parenting | FAMILY & RELATIONSHIPS / Parenting / General
Classification: LCC BV4526.3 .S93 2023 (print) | LCC BV4526.3 (ebook) | DDC 248.4—dc23/eng/20220919
LC record available at https://lccn.loc.gov/2022034711
LC ebook record available at https://lccn.loc.gov/2022034712

Published in association with The Bindery Agency, www.TheBinderyAgency.com.

Cover design: Faceout Studio, Spencer Fuller
Interior design: Denise Froehlich

Printed in the United States of America

22 23 24 25 26 LBC 5 4 3 2 1

To my amazing parents, Monte and Teddi Hester—Dad, who told me I could do anything in the world I set my mind to but the most important thing I could ever do is to be a great wife and mother . . . and Mom, who showed me what that looks like.

And to Dave's dad, Lyn Swanson, and in memory of his mother, Karin Swanson, who together raised the amazing man I get to do life with.

CONTENTS

FOREWORD

When my husband, Willie, and I first met, there was no way we could have imagined all that was ahead for us. The day we got married, all we knew was that we loved each other and hoped to one day grow a family that would honor God. If someone had told us then that we would raise six children, that we would one day have a reality television show about our family, that we would travel the world and have the opportunity to influence millions through ministry and social media, we would have laughed. (Well, first we would have asked what a reality TV show and social media were. It was 1992!)

While being new parents is never easy, with all our hearts Willie and I believed that God's Word had the wisdom we needed to raise our kids well. We'd been shown that example in the lives of our families of origin, and we still believe it today. While we never parented perfectly, we kept returning to God's principles and trusted in his guidance as we raised each child. Now as we're beginning to see the next generation come up in our grandbabies, we could not be more convinced that God knows what he's doing and that his ways are always better than what we could ever imagine!

I met Monica when I came on her podcast to talk about my book *Strong and Kind: Raising Kids of Character.* As we spoke that day, I knew that though we lived across a continent and one big ocean from each other, Monica and I shared a heart for raising kids who love Jesus and love each other. Kids of character and faith. Mine grew up riding four-wheelers, and Monica's grew up riding waves, but we shared the same goal of pointing our children to the true meaning of success: loving God and loving others. Praying that our children would stay in the center of God's will, wherever he might place them.

Willie and I always told our kids that no matter what they did, if they were following God and staying true to his Word, they could trust him to lead them. True success is to live a life that pleases our heavenly Father, a life that exudes the fruits of the Spirit: love, joy, peace, patience, kindness, gentleness, faithfulness, and self-control. This is done in the small things just as much as in the big ones. Nothing makes us prouder than seeing our kids live lives that honor God, whether or not anyone sees them doing it!

Recently, Monica's son Luke won the World Junior Surfing Championships. I saw his post-win interview, and I loved hearing him say to the camera, "Before the final, my mom texted me to remind me that when I win, I need to remember to thank God." I love that he gave credit to his mom in that moment but even more importantly that he gave the glory to God. That's what true success looks like!

Only God knows what our kids will grow up to be or do, but what a joy it is to partner with him in the process. And what a gift that he gives us other women and men to encourage and inspire us to keep doing the good, hard work of parenting. We all may be separated by miles or hills or oceans, but I hope you read this book—as Monica and her husband share their stories and offer wisdom from God's Word to help you along—as though it's a virtual mentor. Whether you're just getting started or are smack-dab in the middle of parenting, I'm over here cheering for you and believing that God will lead as you're busy raising your own amazing kids!

Korie Robertson

Three Important Things—and a Special Word to Dads

Hi, friends! I'm so happy you're opening this book, and I pray you'll be blessed as you read it.

I want to make three things super clear before you dive into the chapters ahead. Also, I know most of you are likely moms, but I want you and the dads reading to know there's definitely something here for the men too.

First, about the Title—*Amazing?*

Am I really suggesting that we should try to raise amazing kids? I mean, aren't most of us simply trying to survive here? Like let's keep them alive, out of jail, and on track to graduate from high school, right? Isn't "amazing" a little . . . extra? A bit over the top?

I hear you. But, yes, I really do mean it. With all my heart, I do! First, your kids *are* amazing, because they were made in the image of the most amazing God. No matter their challenges or struggles, your kids are eternal beings who have the potential to honor God with the life they've been given. I may not know them personally, but I'm already cheering for your kids. And for you, their parents, too.

When I use the word *amazing*, I am talking about kids who are strong in character and conviction. Kids who know God's truth and how to stand for it and on it. Kids who are humble and kind, who walk in integrity. Kids who face adversities and might even fall down a time or twenty but then get back up with courage and faith.

Further, I'm convinced that as parents, we have more influence over our kids and their future than a lot of people want us to believe. I know, I know—our kids have a free will, and we can't dictate their future choices. But whatever age your kids are or whatever stage they're in, there's a lot you *can* do to help them grow up to find and fulfill their greatest potential. That's what this book is all about.

But it's essential that we're clear on the definition of the "amazing" we're working with in this book:

> **AMAZING:** A pleasant surprise; something that causes wonder.[1]

That! That is what we're shooting for here. We want to raise kids who shine like stars in the night sky. Kids who are a pleasant surprise in our increasingly dark world. Kids like this are sure to make people wonder. And then we can hope that wonder will point people to the amazing God behind it all.

As parents, we have more influence over our kids and their future than a lot of people want us to believe.

You'll find three themes throughout this book. Since my book *Boy Mom: What Your*

Son Needs Most from You came out in 2019, these are the three topics I've been asked about the most:

1. **Kids and faith.** God created us all to know him, and kids who grow up in a relationship with Jesus have a solid foundation for an amazing life. This is the most important thing I can share with anyone. (If you're not a spiritual person, I hope you'll read on anyway. I think you'll still get a lot out of the topics here. And I hope what you read gives you reason to consider God's love and plan for you and your family.)
2. **Family relationships.** If you follow me on social media or have read my blog, you probably know that one of my favorite things to talk about is the strong friendships in our family. They're such a joy, and I wish the same for all of you.
3. **Character.** Character is a huge key to everything we most want for our kids, and it's a topic I've researched a lot. While the topic can seem overwhelming, I do my best to make it simple, practical, and achievable.

These three themes and more will be covered in the chapters ahead.

About Those Dishes . . .

The subtitle for this book mentions kids doing dishes *without being asked.* This grew out of conversations in my family when at some point we all began to connect doing dishes with good character. (I mean, does anyone *want* to do the dishes? Is anything more humble or more generous than doing the dishes without being asked?) Obviously, the point isn't necessarily doing the dishes but the heart behind doing them. Our goal is to raise each of our kids into a young man or woman who has a servant's heart and doesn't shrink back from doing hard things. And ordinary daily tasks, like washing a sink full of dishes, are often the training ground to get them there.

Note: I invite you to share via social media your own kids' shining moments of doing dishes and other amazing things using #raising amazing (see resource section for more info). I can't wait to cheer each other on as we go!

Second, about Fame-and-Fortune Amazing

Ah, yes. Some of you picked up this book because you're hoping to raise uber-successful world changers, kids who win gold medals in the Olympics, or invent the next smart-something, or discover the cure for cancer. I'm so glad you're here! Yes, this is for you too.

Personally, I love the idea of raising kids who will do big things in this world. I'm a go-getter by nature. One of our family mottos is "Go big or go home." When my oldest son, Josiah, was eight and said he wanted to invent flying cars, I said, "Then get started!"

When at ten years old my son Luke said he wanted to be a world champion surfer, I said, "I believe you will be!" (and as I finish writing this book, he just won the Junior World champs!) When my son Jonah was determined to raise his SAT scores enough to get a college scholarship, I said, "Go for it!" (No, that's not true. I actually told him it wouldn't happen, but you can read that story in chapter 10, and I apologized to him later.)

The point is I love cheering on kids to shoot for the stars and do great things, and I think we should be our kids' biggest fans.

But doing big things is not the heart of this book. And it's certainly not the heart of my parenting. In fact, while worldly success is often the by-product of a character-rich life—and most of the pro athletes and high-achieving people we follow credit hard-earned character qualities for their success—that's not the goal here.

If you ask any of my kids (and you'll hear from each of them throughout this book), they'll tell you that my husband, Dave, and I are enthusiastically focused first and foremost on their relationship with God and their character. We're more concerned with who they are than with what they'll do. We're more interested in their having a strong walk with God than anything else, and we cheer them on to follow him wholeheartedly. We also know that, often, a life yielded to God's plan is a quiet and modest life. Nothing could make me prouder than raising kids who grow up to honor God with their sincere devotion to him and stay committed for a lifetime.

Third, about My Not Perfect Family

Dave and I have four sons. The first three are somehow legal adults now! As I write this introductory note, Josiah, twenty-two, will be graduating from Westmont College this year with a major in data analytics. Jonah, twenty, is a sophomore at Westmont College, studying engineering. Luke, eighteen, is about to graduate from high school and is already a professional surfer. He'll be taking online college classes while chasing his dreams.

So far, all three are truly amazing young men of character and faith. We still homeschool Levi, our twelve-year-old, who's also a surfer but has recently become passionate about playing golf. I've still got a lot of parenting ahead of me, and as I write to you I'm also writing to myself.

You'll hear more from and about all these guys in the chapters ahead, and while I'm very proud of them, I want to be clear that they and their parents are all very much human and nowhere near perfect. We've gone through difficult seasons, and we'll have more of those ahead.

One of my boys recently experienced a challenging season facing health issues and anxiety. It was a scary experience that has stretched us in new ways. But nothing about that makes him any less amazing. In fact, seeing him seek help, trust God with his challenges, and take steps to get better is, in my opinion, about as amazing as it gets.

I'm happy to say that thus far none of our boys have rebelled or turned away from God. I hope hearing that doesn't intimidate you but might inspire you. While I won't be sharing a formula for making that happen (because there isn't one), I will share the biblical principles I believe make it a lot more likely.

I can't predict what the future holds for any of my kids. They're human, and they, too, have that free will thing. But I'm convinced that the choices Dave and I have made and continue to make as parents have and will continue to play a huge role in the direction their lives take. And that is what motivates me.

Grace and Humor

Only one perfect parent exists, and it's not me. Or you. It's God. None of us will get it all right all the time, so it's important that we know and receive God's grace, daily. His goodness is beyond our understanding, and as hard as it might be to believe, he loves our kids even more than we do! Since this book is primarily written to offer practical wisdom and advice, I want to make sure you read all of it through a lens of grace. While I'm calling us all up to a high standard of parenting, please know I'm doing so with utter dependence on God's Spirit to lead and a big dose of his mercy and grace each day.

Finally, I love humor and think it is a key to maintaining our sanity in parenting. I've laughed at internet videos of the hot-mess moms with a carton of ice cream in one hand and a glass of wine in the other, bemoaning motherhood. They're funny. *But I don't want to be them.* And I don't want you moms (and dads) to be them either.

We can do better! We can be both honest about the struggles of parenting and courageous to keep doing our best in the midst of them. We can laugh at life's craziness while taking our role as parents seriously. We can parent with the dignity our high calling deserves. I know the days can be very, very long, but one day you'll see this season of raising kids for what it is: short.

In this book I offer some straightforward, loving messages on why, though it's hard, it's still possible to raise amazing kids in the world today. I get practical. I share my struggles and victories. I share research and biblical truth, and I cheer you on to do the work now so you'll have no regrets later.

Because at the end of your days, nothing will matter more than the legacy you leave behind in the children you've raised.

Can I Get a Quick Word with Just the Dads?

(Waving the guys over for a quick chat.)

Hey, dads. I'm so glad you're here! I want to give you a big high five just for taking the time to read this little note. Even if your wife bribed you, I appreciate your effort.

At the end of each chapter in this book, my husband, Dave, has a few words just for you in a section titled "A Word to Dads." I hope you'll take the time to read them. They're important.

The truth is Dave has helped write every chapter of this book, beginning to end. I'm so grateful for his wisdom and input! But because we know most men, including Dave, don't read a lot of parenting books, we thought it would be helpful if he offered a quick highlight reel just for you. That way, if you don't get to read the whole chapter, you'll get Dave's note with a few encouraging words, man-to-man.

Dave is by profession a hospital doctor who trained in family practice medicine. He's spent years dealing with infections, disease, and countless end-of-life situations. He interacts with families facing difficult news every day, and he's gained solid perspective on what really matters at the end of life.

Dave is also a dude. He grew up in the country in Oregon, played college and a little pro soccer, and would rather watch *Star Wars* on the couch with his sons than go out for a fancy date with me (he'll deny it, but I'm pretty sure). He loves his tractor and his dog, and he doesn't worry much about how he looks or what people think. I think you'll like him.

Dave is also deeply committed to God and knows the Bible very well. He's a wonderful father who should get most of the credit for how our boys are turning out. He leads by example, he loves us well, and I have so much respect for him.

Which leads me to *my* message to you, men: the chapters in this book are for you too. This call to raising amazing is for dads as much as for moms. In the years I've worked in the world of parenting, I've come to know many families and learned a lot about the successes and failures parents face in raising their kids. And when I hear from a mom who's struggling because her son or daughter isn't doing well in any variety of ways, even though she believes she "did everything right," I always ask a few questions.

What I often learn is that Mom did do a great job. Never perfect, but she was all-in. But Dad? At some point the story often goes like this: he checked out—emotionally, spiritually, and often physically. When kids are struggling, there's often a connection to a dad who didn't rise up to lead well or love well.

Dads, your kids need you. They need you to be in the game. Not perfect (none of us are) but invested. Involved. Leading the best you can. They need you to show up. Support them. They need to go to church with you and see you loving their mom well.

I know it's not easy. You're busy. Work is stressful. Marriage is hard work. You might have your own hobbies that provide the stress relief you believe you need. I get it. Dave gets it too, trust me. But he's also learned—sometimes the hard way—how to stay in the game, even when it's hard. And he wants to help you do the same.

So, please, read the chapters in this book but especially tune in to the notes from Dave. They might offer the hope you crave, the tools you lack, and the kick in the butt we all occasionally need. And just so you know, nothing is more attractive to us moms than a dad fully invested in his family.

Our culture is lacking godly leaders, and you're in a position to make a massive difference in the future of your children and our world. Truly. Thanks for being here, and I hope this book is a big encouragement to you!

CHAPTER 1

ALL-IN

Fully Embrace Your Role as Parent

A strong sense of commitment is the foundation
for a strong, fully functional home.
—**Tony Evans**

Our first son was born a whopping nine pounds, one ounce. His size was unexpected, but even more startling was the sight of his newborn body—gray-blue and floppy. I got only a quick look at him before the medical team went into action cutting the umbilical cord and whisking him out of the room and out of my sight. My husband followed on their heels while I was left alone with the obstetrician and a solitary nurse, who awkwardly talked me through the final contractions and afterbirth delivery.

In a state of shock, for ten minutes I wondered if my baby was alive or dead. What just happened? Those minutes seemed an eternity. Finally, a nurse returned with the news that after eight minutes of being bagged with oxygen, my baby took his first breath. I felt great relief along with uncertainty and fear.

The hours that followed were an emotional roller coaster as our son, whom we named Josiah David, had multiple seizures before being emergency transferred to a trauma hospital. I begged to be released, and hours after Josiah was settled in the brightly lit neonatal intensive care unit, I was able to see him. For just a few brief moments, I had the chance to hold him, behind a curtain, skin to skin, wires and cords delicately dangling between little arms and my tear-soaked chest.

Tests were run, blood was drawn, Josiah was placed on sedative medication, and the seizures finally subsided. There were so many questions and very few answers. Dave was in medical school at the time, finishing his second year, and had just enough knowledge to wreak havoc on his new-father heart. Lack of oxygen at birth is often associated with brain damage, and we were only told to "wait and see."

During those days, camped out in a room off the NICU, Dave and I prayed and talked about what the future may hold. I have never felt so dependent on God nor so consumed with another life. With all we knew might lie ahead, one thing was clear: *we were all-in*. This boy was our precious gift, and our role as his parents would now shape much of our purpose. *Whatever that looked like.*

I don't claim to understand how God works and why sometimes prayers are answered one way and other times another way, but in this case Josiah was healed completely. At his six-month appointment, his brain activity was in the normal range. We were incredibly grateful. I loved that baby boy and committed to being the best mom I could ever be to him.

While no pregnancy or delivery is easy, my next three boys came into the world comparatively stress free. I'll never forget those frightening first days with my oldest son, but looking back

I see that, over time, I began to take the amazing miracle each of my children is for granted. A few short years later the everydayness of life with young kids had worn me down, and I found myself overwhelmed with parenting. Instead of counting blessings, I counted the hours until I could get a break from my kids.

The only all-in I felt was the sensation that I was drowning in motherhood. I daydreamed about "real" jobs where I would wear "real" clothes, losing sight of the truth that the greatest job in the world was staring me in the face with peanut butter smears and a superman cape.

What happened to the fully committed feelings I had when my first son was born? Why was it so hard to love these kids well every day?

In the years that followed, I learned that being all-in as a parent has to be more than an emotional response. It requires something higher—a choice made by our will.

(The Right Kind of) Love Is Required

God created man and woman and told us to "be fruitful and multiply." In giving us that command, he also provided us with instincts and impulses that allow us to have babies, then raise them until they can one day be independent.

Within a mother and father is a natural, affectionate love for their children. The Greeks categorized love into various types, and they refer to this kind of parental-affectionate love as "storge" (pronounced with a hard *g*). It is tender, merciful, and emotional. And it's beautiful.

Back when newborn Josiah was in the hospital, I was flooded with storge love. In fact, much of parenting in the early years is based on and motivated by this instinctual love.

Yet storge love won't be sufficient to be "all-in" for all the years we raise our kids and all the challenges that will come our way. To raise kids with excellent character and godly standards in this broken world requires us to choose something higher: a dedication led not by emotions but by a commitment to train up children in the way they should go (Prov. 22:6).

C. S. Lewis refers to this higher way as the Moral Law. In his book *Mere Christianity*, he compares the impulse of a mother's natural love to musical notes: "Think once again of a piano. It has not got two kinds of notes on it, the 'right' notes and the 'wrong' ones. Every single note is right at one time and wrong at another." Lewis goes on to explain the need for something greater: "The Moral Law is not any one instinct or set of instincts: it is something which makes a kind of tune (the tune we call goodness or right conduct) by directing the instincts."[1]

Indeed, I needed—and I still need—the Moral Law, God's law written on my heart to direct my instincts. When the natural affectionate feelings of parental love wear off (because they do), we need to have a commitment that goes deeper and calls us higher. To raise amazing children, we must parent out of something that supersedes emotions. We must make decisions of the will. Bending our will to the truth we know about God's ways, his calling, and eternity.

To be all-in means we're committed to more than just parental instincts; we're committed to principles that will guide our parenting through every season. Through good times and bad, when we're fighting for a life or just fighting to stay awake.

Start with Perspective

Perspective is a game changer. While it's not realistic to live in a perpetual state of parenting bliss, I think we need reminders—daily, if possible—of this great calling. It's one thing to be all-in with a newborn who needs you to fight for his life, but it's quite another to be all-in on a rainy Tuesday with a house full of needy kids. To be all-in for all the years of parenting requires great intentionality—because we humans are forgetful, aren't we? We tend to take things for granted.

One reason I love watching the film *It's a Wonderful Life* every holiday season is that it causes me to reflect on my own life and how easily I, too, tend to lose perspective. If I was given the opportunity to get a flash-forward of how differently life could go depending on a few choices, it might help me make better choices every day.

Appreciate the Privilege and Responsibility

Parenting can feel like an unrelenting, thankless job. The days are long, especially in the early years, and it can be incredibly easy to lose appreciation for the gift of our children and the privilege of parenting them. Then as our kids grow up and gain more independence, we have new options—new temptations—to tune out or check out, to farm out every aspect of our kids' education and spiritual growth and all other activities to others.

We chase our own dreams, build a side hustle, binge Netflix, reinvent our social life, numb ourselves with substances or social media. And then we miss some of the most amazing moments hidden in everyday life with children.

Recently on Instagram, someone shared a photo of three jars with beads in them. Their church had sent the jars home with every child in Sunday school, and the beads represented the number of weekends they had left until high school graduation. This was a visual reminder of how precious time with our children is and how temporary this season of parenting is. I saw the one with only a few beads, lonely, lining the bottom of the jar, which represented my son Luke's timeline.

I cried.

Visual reminders like this make me wonder, "Have I spent enough time with my children? Like, real, intentional time? Have I given them the best of me, or leftovers?" I still have time with Levi, who's now twelve as I write. He wants so much of me—another hug, a back scratch, answers to so many questions, and so much attention. How often do I respond to him with "Mom is busy!" without lifting my eyes from my phone or as I push him out of my room?

And another bead is gone.

Parents, I don't know what helps you recognize the great privilege and responsibility you have as a mom or dad, but we all need to tap into that privilege. These kids in your care? Whether they're seven months or seven years or seventeen, they're a gift to you. And you? You were hand-chosen to be their parents! And no one in the world has more impact on your children than you do as parents. And they crave love from and desire a relationship with no one more than you. Camp out on that for a minute.

I don't write any of this to shame or guilt you. You're hearing it from a mom who has shed real tears over her own parenting regrets. A mom who's good at loving when the emotions are all lined up but has at times failed to rise up when her own comfort or plans are at stake.

No one in the world has more impact on your children than you do.

But as I write this first chapter, I'd like to invite you to join me in committing, whether for the first time or the four-hundredth, to all-in parenting. To an intentional approach to parenting that supersedes emotions and enables you to parent in such a way that your kids will thank you later.

But first let's be clear about four things "all-in" parenting isn't—and then is.

1. *All-in parenting isn't smothering, controlling, helicopter, or snowplow parenting.* It's choosing to provide our kids with a healthy, mature love, offering boundaries and freedoms as they're needed.

2. *All-in parenting isn't losing our personal identity and living a child-centered life 24/7 for eighteen years straight.* It's knowing our job as a parent is one of our highest callings. It's being healthy and wise, secure, and strong as we do our best to make good, sound choices for ourselves and our families. It's being intentional about our priorities, placing God first in our lives, our marriages next, and our children after that. It means making choices in our work, ministry, and community with consideration for how those things will impact our first priorities.

3. *All-in parenting isn't getting our self-worth from our kids' performances or successes.* It's striving for excellence in our parenting while knowing that ultimately our kids have a free will and will have to make their own choices. Our self-worth is found only in our relationship with God.

4. *All-in parenting isn't a formula for how to raise perfect kids.* It's a commitment to following God's principles and wisdom from his Word to the best of our ability, knowing we'll never get it perfect but never giving up, then resting in God's grace and kindness, asking him to reach our kids' hearts.

How to Live as an All-In Parent

You can demonstrate your love for your kids in a thousand ways, but here are eleven ways you can live out your commitment to be all-in for them.

1. **Be present.** Put down your phone. Close your laptop. Tune in and be fully *with* your kids when you're with them. This is harder than it sounds, which leads me to . . .

2. **Listen.** Listening is a discipline most of us aren't very good at. Showing our kids we're interested in all the little stories and recollections of their day (even if it's mostly super important information about Spider-Man or their latest obsession) builds confidence that they have our attention for the bigger things later. Whether or not your child is a talker, keep showing up so they'll realize you're there for them when they need to talk. (Also, teenagers usually decide to talk late at night when you're ready to collapse into bed, but it's worth staying up for.)

3. **Be a person of your word.** All-in parents earn their kids' trust through integrity. This means doing what you say you'll do and being who you say you are. Be careful to promise only what you can fulfill, and if you must break a commitment, take that seriously and own up to it. This not only sets an example for your child but communicates how much you value them.

4. **Adjust your schedule to your family's.** We often work hard because we love our kids and want to provide for them. But if we work so much that we have too little time with them, we need to reconsider our motives. Kids spell love: "T-I-M-E." It won't always be possible to set your own work schedule, but as much as it depends on you, do all you can to give your family as much time as you can. If you can't adjust your work hours, take care to prioritize your off time and be focused on what matters. Also, many families could live on less income if they adjusted their lifestyle, giving the family more time together.

5. **Show up when they need you.** You can't be everywhere, and your kids will understand that. But do your best to be there when they need you most: Mornings and evenings. For the games, shows, and awards. At the principal's office and after the breakup.

6. **Take care of yourself.** Kids need healthy parents. They feel more secure when we're rested, balanced, and happy. In her book *More Than a Mom*, Kari Kampakis said, "Wellness helps you become the best version of yourself so you can bravely and boldly serve God."[2] So true! No one but you can give your kids a happy mom or dad. Make it a priority.

7. **Be all-in in your marriage.** More on this in chapter 5, but it's too important not to include here. A healthy marriage is one of the greatest gifts you can give your children. If you're married, invest in your marriage daily.

8. **Invest in things they love.** Get interested in what interests your kids. If you let them play video games, learn something about the games they love. When our fourth son decided he loved to golf, the sport was foreign to Dave and me. Dave invested time into learning about the game—reading articles and studying the best players. Levi felt his dad's commitment to him through that effort.

9. **Have fun with them.** Next to T-I-M-E, I would say kids spell love F-U-N! The average kid laughs three hundred times a day compared to a measly seventeen times a day for us adults.[3] Laughter connects us and unites us. It builds memories, and it's healthy. Most of all, having fun with our kids shows them we enjoy them, and that fulfills a desire of every human heart.

10. **Give them loving touch.** God made us to need physical touch, and kids crave a parent's affection. Even as they

grow up and may pull away physically, yours will still need your loving touch. I made a "hug a night" rule with my oldest son when he became a teenager, and it was a ritual I think we both needed as he grew into independence.

11. **Humbly ask for forgiveness.**

Want a few more ideas? In the resource section, find a printable list of twenty-five ways to show your kids you're all-in. None of us will get parenting or anything else right all the time. And when we own our mistakes and ask for forgiveness, we're both modeling something important to our kids and showing them that we value and respect them.

So Let's Dive (All) In

When I go into the ocean with my boys, sometimes I just want to cool off but don't want my hair to get wet. So I try to keep my head above the water. They always tease me when I do this, yelling, "You've got to commit, Mom!" and "It's not even worth swimming if you don't go all the way in."

As we close this first chapter, I hope you'll take some time to consider this:

Do you want to merely dip your toes into the parenting waters, do as little as you must until your kids are grown and launched into the world? (It's possible to do this—in fact, it's quite common.) Or do you want to go all-in? Give your kids your best and their best chance at growing up to be exceptional adults down the road. You won't have all the say, we know that. But as far as your role is concerned, are you ready to go all the way in? To get your hair wet and everything?

I hope so!

I'm praying for you and cheering you on for the next fourteen chapters as we look at the most important choices parents get to make when it comes to all-in parenting and as you say yes to intentionally raising your amazing kids.

A Word to Dads

Hey, dads. This is Dave. Besides helping Monica develop the thoughts in this book, my job here is to end each chapter offering a few "dad-specific" words. So this is geared toward you. I'll start by saying I'm glad you're reading *Raising Amazing*. I honestly wish I'd had my hands on good books that dealt with these issues when my kids were younger. But, hey, we can learn from trial and error too.

Parenting isn't easy, and I'm not a perfect dad. But I've learned a lot along the way, and I do hope to encourage you to "dad well." Over time, I've learned that parenting is truly a high calling—the most important job you'll ever have!

As for chapter 1, I hope you've read all of it. Monica shares a big part of our family story, and this chapter represents both of our hearts for parenting. I will tell you honestly that being all-in was a process for me. I might have said I was all-in during the early years, but life was in many ways more all about me. I still had some serious selfishness to shed. I loved my family, but love for my own activities and lifestyle competed with it at times.

When I started medical school, I had so little free time that when I did get a break, I wanted to use it to tune out. Mostly, I wanted time to do what I enjoyed. This was one of the biggest challenges in our marriage, honestly. Monica and I experienced ongoing collisions between my agenda and hers. And I was always trying to squeeze the two together.

The Mother's Day when I snuck in a soccer game on my way home from the hospital knowing that my wife just wanted time with me (or a break from parenting) might have been a low point. I showed up at home without showering, with my work clothes back on, acting like I'd come straight from working at the hospital. My sweat-salted kiss on arrival was a dead giveaway, and then it was Monica who got salty. It wasn't her favorite Mother's Day.

Getting married and growing up is harder for us guys, I think. You may not be tempted to sneak in soccer games, but we all have that thing that begs for our time and attention. It could be doing yard work, fixing up cars, viewing a Netflix series, or watching the stock market or the news. You might serve in ministry or spend extra hours with clients to get an edge on the competition, and these are not bad things. But sometimes it's not about what's good or bad; it's about what's good or better. In an honest moment you know what you put first.

But here's what I've learned: being an all-in dad and a committed husband are the most rewarding jobs I've ever had. At some point I traded in much of my recreation for the more important things. I slowly let go of activities I thought I needed to do and let my wife and kids lead in things they wanted to do.

I didn't grow up with a big interest in skateboarding and surfing, but they're what I learned to support my kids. I learned to give up my time for theirs. I even learned to be a caddy for my youngest, the golfer. I may not be in the kind of shape I once was, but life is much richer this way.

We all need balance, and that means we dads need to get in some recreation. You need that time to hang out with good friends, play, and take care of yourself. But I encourage you to wisely navigate how you spend your time and what you devote yourself to. As a dad, your role requires making it your highest priority to be all-in for your family.

Follow the suggestions Monica outlined above (I helped her with them!) and lean into God when you're frustrated. Jesus was the best model for self-sacrificial love ever, so get to know him and learn his ways. Later in life you won't care how good your golf game was or which buddy you hung out with this weekend, but you will treasure memories of being with your children as they discovered new things in nature, learned to read, won or lost a game, or wrestled with hard questions.

Also, your wife is the best friend you'll ever have, and she'll be the one with you long after the kids are grown and gone. Take good care of her. Your family is God's gift to you, and you are God's hand-picked gift to them. Don't blow it.

Thoughts from Jonah, Age Twenty

Growing up, I've been blessed by my parents' commitment to my brothers and me as well as to each other. From all their schooling and character training to their support in our sports and life endeavors, our parents have truly demonstrated what it means to be "all-in." I'm especially impressed by the fact that for my parents, parenting does not seem like a chore but part of the motion of their lives, which they love and cherish. Obviously, we all get tired, and my parents are by no means perfect, but I've been impressed by the way they've steadfastly demonstrated what it means to be committed to the family in a deep and intentional manner.

Recently, I've witnessed their love for me in a new light. During my sophomore year at college, after a stressful and exhausting semester, I began to experience some health symptoms that triggered anxiety. We still aren't sure what caused all of it, but it took quite a toll on me. When I felt most overwhelmed, my parents flew me home for a break. After some time with them, I was ready to go back, but they continued to support me the best they could through my entire healing process.

I can rest in the fact that my value to my parents isn't based on my school grades, achievements, or strength. They loved me in my most vulnerable state, even though I wasn't feeling like the successful student and strong person I wanted to be for them.

I'm so thankful for the health of my family and for the effort we all put in—kids included—to making us amazing and strong, together. And I think that knowing my parents are all-in provides us with the stable foundation we get to grow from.

Reflection Questions

1. How have I tended to parent out of emotion rather than out of commitment? How might I more consistently tap into the motivation to parent from a place of commitment?

2. What makes me lose perspective in my parenting, and what might I tap into to help remind me of the privilege and blessing of raising my child(ren)?

3. What's one way I might demonstrate my "all-in" commitment to my kids and family this week?

CHAPTER 2

WELCOME ABOARD

Lead Your Family on an Intentional Trajectory

The forces pulling on families are too strong in the modern world. Ultimately, we must decide either to steer, or to go where the river takes us.
—**William Doherty**

Imagine boarding an airplane and the captain saying, "Um, uh, well, welcome aboard. I'm not sure where we're going or how long it will take to get there but buckle up and let's see how it goes." You look around at the fellow passengers, and no one else seems to have a clue either. After takeoff, someone tosses snacks around, but you aren't sure if you should eat them right away or save them for a long flight ahead. After a few minutes of turbulence shakes the plane, the captain comes on again and with a nervous laugh says, "Not sure what that was, but let's hope for the best!"

Sounds like a nightmare, doesn't it?

Compare that to what we normally expect on a flight and how secure I feel when the captain comes on with a friendly, casual tone and says, "Welcome aboard Flight 890 to Honolulu. We'll be traveling for five hours and thirty minutes today. Once we reach our cruising altitude of 38,000 feet, the flight attendants will be serving drinks and a snack. We'll have a few bumps on our initial ascent, but we'll adjust accordingly, and the rest of the trip should be smooth sailing today. Sit back and enjoy."

Big difference, right?

Mom and Dad, when we bring kids into this world, we're essentially welcoming them aboard our family "plane." Yet often, in the busyness of the parenting years, we neglect to make a flight plan, and we may find our normal cruising altitude is full of turbulence. Kids feel insecure when there is a chaotic tone in our homes—when schedules and needs and moods are inconsistent. And when this goes on long enough, kids start looking elsewhere for a sense of security and identity.

Yet what a difference for a child growing up with parents who have set their trajectory intentionally. How much more secure a child will feel when Mom and Dad can tell them confidently, "You're a part of this family. You belong here! This is who we are, and this is where we're headed. *You can trust us.*" When these families hit the unavoidable turbulence of life, the parents say, "We knew there would be bumps, but we also know how to get through them. And we'll do it together."

Parents, your kids need a leader, and God has hand-picked you for the job.

Parents, the first step in raising amazing children is to put on your captain's hat. Your kids need a leader, and God has hand-picked you for the job.

Choose to Lead Your Family with Intention

We tend to easily invest a lot of time and intentional effort into many areas of life. We're strategic about academic and job deadlines, we follow workout schedules to accomplish fitness goals, and we carve out time to organize our financial plans, vacation plans, and meal plans. Yet we often neglect to be intentional with our own family—the most important part of our lives! We tend to face parenting and family life as though everything will fall into place naturally. And while that would be nice, it just doesn't work that way.

Here's the truth: amazing kids grow out of amazing families. And amazing families don't happen by chance. They're formed by prayerful planning, sacrifice, determination, sweat, and most often, more than a few tears.

If you've ever encountered a family that just seems like they've got it all together—they're happy and secure, they get along, they have a sense of purpose and direction about them—I can assure you this did not happen by chance. Families like this are the product of parents who intentionally lead their kids with purpose.

Amazing kids grow out of amazing families. And amazing families don't happen by chance.

That's what I want for you and me. So let's talk about how to get there. Though all our families are unique, here are three steps toward building amazing families on purpose.

1. Know Your Identity

A secure identity is foundational to our faith and personal fulfillment. Dave and I work hard to help our kids grow up to be secure in their individual identity as God's children so they might avoid the pitfalls of false identities the world is guaranteed to throw at them. Feeling confident in our identity is crucial to a healthy spiritual life and for navigating our time on this planet. (We'll talk more about kids and identity in chapter 14.)

As parents, we have the awesome opportunity to also raise our kids with an understanding of their *family identity*. We are *all* God's children (yep, even Mom and Dad!), and he's placed us all in our unique families *on purpose*. Together, families get to develop an identity uniquely their own.

We can refer to our unique family identity as our family culture.

A growing emphasis in businesses has been developing their brand's "culture." Chick-fil-A, the most popular fast-food chain in America on a per-location basis, is known for their stellar customer service. For example, my sons love to eat at Chick-fil-A and are always eager to offer the employees a "thank you," anticipating the famous "My pleasure!" response. Consistent gestures like this have set the tone for a unique and positive customer experience.

Business Insider said, "Chick-fil-A thrives because customers value the pleasant dining experience they have come to count on from the restaurant, an experience that likely results from the top-down corporate culture of the company." It also said that those leading the company determined that this would be their company identity and they trained their employees to follow.[1]

Like businesses, every family has a culture that's unique. Your family culture is made up of the values, priorities, and routines that define your days, your home, and your life. If you're young and trendy, you might call it your family "brand." I like to say it's what gives our families their unique flavor!

Similar to a business, those families who impress us with their character and connectedness are most often the result of top-down culture. Parents set the tone; kids follow.

The truth is we communicate our family values and culture every day—with or without putting it into words. The way you speak, spend money and time, and relate to people and possessions all give your kids a message about who you are as a family. And here's the thing: if you haven't put thought into your family culture, then you've created one by default. And I probably don't need to tell you *it could be better.*

In an article on fathering, Brett and Kate McKay wrote,

> Family cultures created by default are just like their business culture counterparts: mediocre. Parents haven't thought through what kind of values they want to impart to their kids, and just figure that those values, as well as close bonds between family members, will just happen as the years go by. They then wonder why their kids didn't turn out the way they had vaguely imagined and hoped for, but never articulated or planned out.[2]

I don't want mediocre for my family, and I bet you don't either. There's a lot at stake here!

Personally, I think this process can be a lot of fun. Whereas you had little say in the environment of the family you grew up in, as parents now leading your own family, you get to choose. This is your chance to craft the family of your dreams.

2. Start with Values

A great exercise in articulating your family identity and culture is to gather a list of your family's core values. If your kids are young, this is a great time for you to clarify who you want to become as your family grows. It's never too early to start! If your kids are older, bring them into this conversation.

Here are a few questions each family member might respond to as you get started:

- What are the core values that define our family? What do we really care about?
- How would we hope others might describe us?
- What is your favorite thing about our family? What do you look forward to coming home to?
- What are some things that give us "flavor," specific interests, hobbies, gifts, challenges that make us different from other families?
- How do we like to spend our time together? Are we adventurers or book lovers? Travelers or homebodies? Do we love to cook or garden, build things or listen to music?

There are no wrong answers here; give your family permission to gather everyone's thoughts and be sure to jot them down. Also, remind one another that this is your real list, not one "fit" for social media or suitable for publicity. Sadly, in the world we live in today, we can find ourselves crafting a family image that isn't reality. That's not what this is about. In fact, your list may be kept totally private for just your family, so keep it real!

At the same time, I encourage you to be visionary. Perhaps you value service but realize you haven't been very active in serving others. Or you've always wanted to plant a garden, but you haven't gotten around to it. Your list might include values you want to commit to over time.

These are powerful first steps in shaping an intentional family culture. Have fun with this!

3. Adjust and Embrace

Your family may look different from how you once imagined. You may live with a medical challenge or tight finances. Perhaps you're a single parent (or feel like one). You might live in a location or circumstance you wouldn't have chosen. Acknowledge that, and allow the kids to voice their honest feelings as well. You might pray through these hard things as you choose to trust that God is sovereign, even in the disappointing or difficult things. He cares so much about our families, and our feelings don't surprise him.

Even in the midst of your less-than-ideal circumstances, God has an ideal for you. It's found in a faith walk where he works all things together for your good and his glory (Romans 8:28). He is trustworthy! His ways are always best.

My brother's son was diagnosed with Duchenne Muscular Dystrophy when he was just a toddler. DMD is a genetic condition that promises a difficult life with the average lifespan ending in the early- to mid-twenties. This diagnosis was a massive blow to my brother's family. Though the news was heartbreaking, I've watched my brother rise to be the best dad he can be. He learned all he could about DMD, joined committees, and became an advocate for other DMD families. Running marathons and hosting fundraisers for DMD research has shaped much of his family culture and brought greater awareness of this horrific disease to others who have come alongside them in the battle.

Many factors might shape your family. Once you've gathered a list of your family's core values and unique traits, you're ready to set your intentions on how these will play out in practical ways.

Set Your Trajectory

In their book *Family Shift*, Rodney and Michelle Gage note, "Every family ends up somewhere, but few families end up somewhere on purpose."[3] It's time to clarify where in the world you're headed.

I often think of Zig Ziglar's quote, "Aim for nothing and you'll hit it every time." And wise King Solomon penned the proverb, "Where there is no vision, the people perish" (Proverbs 29:18 KJV). Essentially, your kids are looking to you to tell them just where this plane is headed. Our families need us to establish and communicate our vision, and one way we can cast this vision is by creating a family mission statement.

Develop a Family Mission Statement

Now, if you feel like I once did—that a family mission statement sounds contrived or corny—don't run off! Like I was, you might be pleasantly surprised by this concept.

A family mission statement is a way to clarify your family's values and trajectory. It unifies your family and gives every member a sense of purpose and meaning. Perhaps one of the best parts is that it can work as a filter to help you make decisions and guide your family in all you'll face ahead.

Stephen Covey defines a family mission statement in his book *The 7 Habits of Highly Effective Families*: "A family mission statement is a combined, unified expression from all family members of what your family is all about—what it is you really want to do and be—and the principles you choose to govern your family life."[4]

Covey also took the pressure off by suggesting, "A mission statement doesn't have to be some big, formal document. It can even be a word or a phrase, or something creative and entirely different such as an image or a symbol."[5]

Our family put off creating a family mission statement until my oldest son was home from college for his first Christmas break (better late than never!). But I was happy to find that as we gathered in the living room after dinner one night, with dry erase marker and whiteboard ready, everyone had fun with the process. I was also relieved to find that even though we hadn't yet written our values on a posterboard, it was apparent that we'd communicated our values and purpose well over the years. We seemed to have a unified sense of who we were as we officially formed our statement.

Here's what our family came up with:

The Swansons live to know Christ,
To love him and serve our neighbors,
To pursue righteousness, integrity, and
excellence in all things,
And to enjoy God's creation and be a part of its
flourishing.

I asked my email community about their family mission statements. Here are two examples from what people shared:

- We, [the family's name], strive to glorify Jesus through our love for him, each other, and those around us. We strive in unity to serve with grace, honesty, kindness, patience, and joy.
- We believe in . . . the power of prayer, trusting God's plan, spreading kindness, expressing gratitude, living with intention, standing up for what is right, serving others, dreaming big, giving our best effort, hugging too much, and living without regrets.
- Another family sent me their family "creed," which the children say from memory every morning:

——— FAMILY CREED ———

1. God has given me self-discipline. I delay gratification.
2. I do all things with excellence.
3. I think of and serve others, over myself with kindness.

- Some families choose a simple statement or theme to live by: "The Hanes do hard things well." "The Carlsons live by faith and not by sight."

There are no rules! You can make your family statement as simple or complex as you like. Note: If you want a simple way to get started, find a "Family Mission Statement Template" in the resource section. Download it and use it as a springboard to create your own family mission statement!

Some families post their mission statement, creed, or list of values in a visible place so they'll be reminded of it often. The key is that this is a vision communicated to and hopefully embraced by all members of the family.

Once you've established a secure identity and know where you're headed, the next practical step is to allow these things to inform your family's daily decisions, priorities, and calendars. As you make plans, let your mission statement be an objective guide.

For example:

- How should we spend our family vacation time this year? What lines up best with what we value and want to shape our family?
- What family rules can we agree on related to technology or entertainment?
- Which charities do we want to support?

You can also use your family mission statement as a filter for parenting decisions. Managing a lot of rules is never fun, so using your agreed-on values or mission as a filter can take the pressure off you and keep decisions more objective. It can also help your kids understand the "why" behind your rules.

- At what age will we allow our kids to have a smartphone or be on social media?
- How do we respond to an invitation for a child to go to a party, concert, or sleepover?

Set Routines and Habits in Motion

When you know what matters most to your family, you can start setting up daily routines that support your mission. This is a great way to determine if you're being realistic with the values you've listed.

If faith is central to your family, how are you living that out practically? If your family values adventure, what are you doing to build adventure into your calendar? Your family might raise funds to serve on a mission trip together or open your home to foster children. You might volunteer at ball games or commit to being on a board or committee for a cause you believe in. But one thing is for sure: if you don't live out what you claim defines you, your mission statement is just words on a whiteboard.

Your actions will reveal how badly you want something. In his book *Atomic Habits*, James Clear writes about the importance of being honest with ourselves as we consider whether or not we live out the things we claim are priorities. Clear says, "Every action you take is a vote for the type of person you wish to become."[6]

Mom and Dad, today is a new day. If you look at your family life thus far and realize you haven't set your trajectory well, it's not too late! God's mercies are new every morning (Lam. 3:22–23), and he's cheering you on to a fresh start. Often quoted, Jim Rohn said, "You cannot change your destination overnight, but you can change your direction overnight." I love that!

Take the time you need to get clear on your family's identity and intentionally set your trajectory. Look back over that plane you're flying and see those passengers, whether they number one, two, or ten. These people are worth it.

Now put on your captain's hat and lead this family well!

A Word to Dads

Okay, dads. There's no escaping it. This is where you've got to step up to the plate—or in keeping with Monica's plane analogy, get into the cockpit. Your family needs someone to fly the plane and help keep it on course. And God has designed you with qualities that make you an ideal candidate for this. Don't take your hands off the yoke. There's no autopilot on this one. Your wife and kids need you to pay attention to what's ahead and stick with the flight plan.

What does "setting" the trajectory look like from day to day? As we'll talk about more in the faith chapter (chapter 4), make it start with God and his Word. In a way, his Spirit is your copilot. And his word acts like a compass; he's helping you with the course corrections. (By the way, isn't it good to know you're not alone up front steering this plane?)

So as you fly, make time for compass checks, and include your family! Be intentional. It's so important to get on the overhead and remind the family what airline you're on, what kind of plane it is, and where it's going. Monica and I have found that choosing a weekly time to round everyone up and gather on the couch for fifteen to twenty minutes to discuss what God is teaching us from his Word is an awesome catalyst for moving our family in the right direction.

It's amazing what happens when we all gather in one place, look around at one another, and realize, *Hey, we're all travel companions!* We'll ask things like, "What did God teach you this week in his Word or as you trusted him with a particular situation?" Or "How did God speak to your heart through a person or circumstance?" We compare notes on how God is working in our lives. We read God's Word. And as we do, in a collective way we begin to better understand whose we are and where we're going.

One thing to note: when you're midflight, it can seem like not much is happening. You're just cruising through the air, and it's quiet. But if you can get a peek into the cockpit, you'll see there's a captain there at the wheel, and he's looking ahead to the horizon and checking all his controls to make sure everything's on course. He's communicating with the control tower as he needs to.

Sometimes, and probably most of the time, that's what your wife and kids need. They need to know you're present and your hand is on the wheel. That you're communicating with God on the family's behalf. Just be there, Dad. It's hard and easy at the same time, but when you do this, your family will have a sense of security knowing they're headed somewhere. Even if you're not sure where you're headed all the time, it's OK. God does, and as long as you follow him, he'll lead all of you.

Thoughts from Levi, Age Twelve

Being the youngest Swanson, I've been growing up knowing what our family is all about. It's like I was born and some things were already decided.

For example, every morning I see people start their day

by reading the Bible. Everyone in the family does sports or at least gets exercise. My brothers and my dad talk about the Bible and about Marvel movies. My mom writes and podcasts and takes too many pictures. Everyone laughs a lot, and my mom cooks healthy food. Even if I didn't like all that (at least the healthy food sometimes), I definitely knew what it meant to be a Swanson from a young age.

My brothers all surf, so I grew up surfing too. A lot of people assumed I'd want to be a pro surfer like my older brother, but I didn't. So when I started golfing last year, it was kind of weird. But my parents supported it, and now everyone is learning about golf, we all talk about golf, and everyone is proud of me. I'm even teaching my older brothers about golf. It feels good to think I've added something new to who the Swansons are. My parents tell me that's how families are put together. Everyone adds something to the family, and we're all important to the family. I like that.

Reflection Questions

1. If I were to describe our current family life like an airplane flight, what kind of flight would that be?

2. What are some of the values I think we're currently building our family on? Would family members agree with me?

3. What values or direction would I like to bring into our family life to help us get on a trajectory that aligns with God's best for us?

CHAPTER 3

PARENTAMORPHOSIS

Model an Amazing Life

Children have never been very good at listening to their elders, but they have never failed to imitate them.

—James Baldwin

One of my favorite sets of TV commercials is for Progressive Insurance. They feature Dr. Rick, "parenta-life coach," whose job it is to help new homeowners *not turn into* their parents. The commercials show him coaching his clients to "come back" after falling into patterns they learned from Mom and Dad. If you haven't seen these, be sure to look them up online. But you can imagine the topics are plenty—from challenges using smartphones to home décor issues and travel quirks.

Dr. Rick says, "You wouldn't believe what can trigger the parent inside of us." He calls it "parentamorphosis."

Each of the commercials end with a spokesperson saying,

"Progressive can't save you from becoming like your parents, but we can save you money when you bundle home and auto insurance with us."

People love these commercials, and for one good reason: they're funny because they're true. Progressive knows what each of us needs to keep in mind as we aim to raise amazing kids: no matter what we teach, preach, or beseech, our kids are more likely to emulate the ones who raised them. Kids will internalize the way they see us living. And that means the best way for us to raise amazing kids is to live an amazing life in front of them.

That sounds easy enough, right?

Not exactly. Most of us can be amazing . . . *now and then*. When we need to be. We might show our best side in front of certain people or during parts of our work or public life. But our kids? They see us, like, *all the time!* Day and night. Before our first cup of coffee in the morning and when we're all dressed up for an evening out. There's no hiding who we are from our kids; they get the real deal.

Young kids are unfiltered, likely to repeat just about anything their parents say. At a recent gathering with other moms, I heard one woman telling her friends she was shocked to hear her five-year-old cuss. "Where in the world did he get that?" she exclaimed, only to have one of her close friends laugh and call her out. I've been called out myself, even if privately, when my son has acted irritated at small things or made rude comments about the tourists slowing down our island traffic. Before I correct him, I stand corrected myself.

As our kids grow up, they become more discerning, keeping family sins—I mean, secrets—to themselves a bit better. But let's not be fooled. Our children aren't only taking in everything they see us do and say. These kids are tucking away our habits, attitudes, and expressions for their own parentamorphosis down the road. *You've been warned.*

But don't let that scare you off. In fact, I want you to consider it a great opportunity!

Modeling an Amazing Life for Your Kids

The truth is I can't live an amazing life for more than five minutes on my own. But the good news is that as I follow Christ, I get to share some of his amazing with the world. I think of the apostle Paul's words in 1 Corinthians 11:1: "Follow my example, as I follow the example of Christ." I want to be able to say that to my kids. None of us will be perfect, but we can raise the bar for ourselves as we set an example for the children we're raising.

Note: Find a printable with 1 Corinthians 11:1 on it in the resource section. Post it somewhere you'll see it often and be encouraged to model well for your kids.

First, Reflect

Before we consider our influence on our children, we're wise to hit pause and take an honest look back. How much of how we parent is a subconscious reflection of our own parents' example? (Gulp.) Grab hold of your imaginary Dr. Rick and consider the good, the bad, and the quirky traits that are undeniably a shadow of your own folks.

Have you carried some things into your family without much thought simply because it's how you grew up? Have you held on to routines and habits, values and priorities that might be more inherited than purposeful? Maybe some of these things are worth questioning. Some of us might tend to overindulge our kids on birthdays or at Christmastime, not because we believe it is right but because it's how we experienced Christmas in our family of origin. Or perhaps we withhold praise from our kids because our parents did not praise us regularly.

Perhaps your parenting style is a reaction to some part of your childhood you disliked and fear repeating. If you were raised with a super-controlling parent, you might catch yourself erring on the side of giving your kids too many freedoms too soon—or vice versa. Keep these things in check. (And don't hesitate to talk to a counselor or therapist to help sort through areas you need help with.)

It's fair to acknowledge that many of us hope to be like our parents in at least some ways. I hope my husband and I are like our own parents in a lot of ways. Yet most of us can think of areas from our childhood we want to improve on for our own kids. There's always hope for change, and the first step is awareness. Decide, on purpose, which parts of your upbringing belongs in the legacy you hope to pass on to your kids.

The Little Things Add Up

Now let's consider nine areas where what you do is likely to be passed on to the next generation. This list isn't comprehensive, but it ought to be a good springboard for some personal reflection.

> *One of the most challenging parts of raising character-rich kids is realizing how much of their character rests on the character we model.*

Your Lifestyle

How you eat, drink, take care of yourself, and choose entertainment will all be stamped on your kids' subconscious. Where do you turn when you're stressed? And how do you celebrate when you're happy? These things matter. Here are some questions that relate to a few areas that have challenged me personally. They might be worthy of self-evaluation.

- Are the TV shows and movies you watch edifying and inspiring? Are you setting a good example for your kids by the entertainment you choose?
- What is your relationship with alcohol? Do you "need" it to relax? Is the way you relate to alcohol or other substances the way you hope your kids will one day?
- What is your relationship with food and exercise? Do you care for your body as God's temple, nourishing it with healthy food and movement? Do your kids hear you speak positive messages about your body, or do you put yourself down or obsess over your physical appearance? If food, your body, or exercise have become idols, there's no doubt it will impact your kids in one way or another.

This is not about perfection but the direction you're going. We're all human, and, indeed, kids will have the opportunity to make choices for themselves as they grow up. But the imprint of parental lifestyle will always be there.

The good news is you can decide to make changes anytime. In fact, if there's an area you realize needs adjusting, allow your kids to inspire you to do the work now. The example you set by working to change may be one of the greatest parenting moves you make.

Your Speech

The words and expressions you use often will be some of the first evidence of modeling you'll see in your kids. Like the mom whose friend called her out for her son's swearing, it will be hard for you to deny that your kids are using words or phrases they learned from you.

My dad has always had the gift of encouragement. He has a way of making anyone in his presence feel important. He looks for specific qualities in people to point out and appreciate, and he especially looks for ways to help and encourage those in need. As a young girl, I found myself often sticking up for the kids being bullied or befriending the new kids in school. This came naturally to me because it was modeled in my home.

We can use our words to build others up or tear them down. To speak life or death. We can encourage and inspire or discourage and frustrate. There's no doubt that if we tell our kids to speak kindly of others, but they hear us gossip and criticize, they're learning more from what we do than from what we say. Yet a child who's raised by a life-speaking, encouraging parent will be likely to grow up to be the same.

Choose your words well, Mom and Dad. They matter in so many ways.

YOUR EMOTIONAL HEALTH AND ANGER

I didn't know I had anger issues until I was raising young children. Unfortunately, parenting can put us in the pressure cooker and bring out our worst. Add to that the fact that we tend to feel safe knowing that our children love us, need us, and are typically quick to forgive us. (I hate to admit I've taken advantage of that more times than I want to remember.)

I'll always regret some of my angry outbursts when my boys were young. One thing I don't regret, however, is reaching out for help because I knew it wasn't healthy. I found a good counselor and opened up to friends who prayed for me and held me accountable to learning how to handle my emotions better.

If you struggle with anger, depression, or any other emotional or mental health issue, I urge you to do something about it. Seek help right away, both for your sake and for the sake of your children. Simply seeking help is modeling what you hope your kids will do if one day they have a challenge they need help with. Talk to a doctor, a pastor, or a trusted friend. Get counseling. You are not alone. As a recovered angry mom, I've been happy to hear that my boys have very few memories of an angry mom. (God's mercies are great!)

YOUR CHARACTER AND INTEGRITY

I talk a lot about raising kids of character, but I will never say it's an easy task. One of the most challenging parts of raising character-rich kids is realizing how much of their character rests on the character we model.

When my youngest son was an infant, I made a hurried trip to Walmart with all four boys in tow. I don't even like Walmart, so a trip there with four little boys was not my idea of fun. I was more than glad to finish shopping and have everyone loaded back up in the car.

Just as I sat down, I looked in my rearview mirror and saw one of my boys reach into his pocket and pull out a pack of gum—along with a big, mischievous grin. I still think he knew we hadn't paid for the gum and his guilty conscience compelled him to reveal the evidence before I left the parking lot.

Oh, how I wanted to ignore the situation. I'm pretty sure I thought of ten different reasons why driving away at that moment would be justified. But I also knew if I let that little illegal act go, I would be setting a wrong standard for my boys. So back inside went the four of us to confess to the Walmart cashier and return the gum (then back home to chat about what just went down).

All the little things you do—how you treat cashiers and food servers, the way you react to other drivers or speak to telemarketers, the way you respond to the hurting or the hurtful—give your kids messages about how you want them to live.

If kids hear you tell white lies, you're communicating that lying is OK. When our kids were little, we would pack the whole family into a cheap hotel room for an occasional "staycation" in Waikiki. It didn't make sense to get a second room, plus we couldn't afford it. Yet one day when I asked two of my boys to stand off to the side (basically, hide) while we checked in, they asked why, and I wasn't sure what to tell them. The truth I could have said was *Because Mommy is lying to the hotel about how many people are going to stay in our room.*

Dave and I had some things to think through. Integrity is hard!

YOUR ATTITUDE AND MINDSET

Mom and Dad set the tone in their home. This is a big responsibility. While I don't suggest we be phony or hide a challenging day, I do think we should model how to best handle hard times. Do we do the work of taking our thoughts captive and using restraint with our words? Or is our default to grumble and complain?

We want our kids to have a growth mindset, believing they can conquer challenges and come through hard times as happier, healthier, more mature people. Are we modeling this? Do you speak negatively about your own life, job, or future? Kids are taking all of this in!

YOUR FRIENDSHIPS

We all need friends, and I hope you have some good ones. In fact, I strongly urge parents to intentionally carve out time to spend with people who offer refreshing fellowship and much-needed laughter.

When we busy parents finally get the chance to hang out with a good friend, however, sometimes we let down our guard. We might tend to "regress." Old stories come up, gossip goes down easy, and oftentimes kids nearby are more tuned in than we're aware. Once again, this scenario has mostly reminded me to raise my own bar: to watch my talk and aim to live—and speak—above reproach.

As I offer my sons wisdom on choosing good friends and influences (see chapter 6), I want to make sure they see me being wise about influences in my own life. Am I intentional about the people I surround myself with? Am I only spending time with people just like me, or do I seek to cross faith and cultural barriers to connect with people I might learn from and build bridges to? Do my kids see me seeking opportunities to live out the Great Commission of Matthew 28, sharing my faith regularly? I know I can improve in all these areas. And this leads us to the next area . . .

YOUR FAITH

One of the biggest responsibilities I feel is to show my kids what a genuine relationship with God looks like. Kids are quick to recognize when their parents are hypocrites, and the last thing I want is to feel responsible for my own children turning away from God because I showed them a lousy picture of what that genuine relationship looks like!

I'm convinced that one of the greatest keys to raising kids to embrace a genuine faith is for their parents to model a genuine faith. Charles Spurgeon once said, "Train up a child in the way he should go, but be sure you are going that way too." We'll talk more about that in the next chapter.

YOUR RELATIONSHIP WITH TECHNOLOGY

Ouch. Did I just step on someone's toes? (*wink*) This one hits way too close to home for me. We'll dive deeper into this topic in chapter 12, but suffice it to say, your scrolling is modeling! Most of us need to set some serious boundaries for ourselves in this area of technology before we stress out about our kids. Experts suggest we put our phones away certain hours of the day. Observe a weekly technology Sabbath. Maybe we can determine that when kids are around the screens are not?

Ponder this one, then do what you need to do to set an amazing example for your kids.

HOW YOU MANAGE MONEY

Money can be a complicated topic, and (thankfully) there are experts and resources available to help guide you in raising kids with good financial sense. I confess this is an area that Dave and I could have done better in with our older boys. I'm grateful for the helpful resources and mentors that filled in some gaps for us, but I do hope to be more intentional with our youngest!

The 11th Annual Parents, Kids & Money Survey done by T. Rowe Price reported that nearly half of parents said they missed opportunities to talk to their kids about money and finances.[1] A quarter of the parents said they were very reluctant or extremely reluctant to discuss financial topics with their children. Even more, half the kids surveyed said they wished their parents taught them more about money.[2]

Indeed, we should teach our kids about money management—saving and spending, giving and generosity. But whether or not we communicate it verbally, our kids are picking up on all the subtle (or not so subtle) ways we spend, talk about, and manage money.

In an article on MoneySense, Karen Robock writes, "While money habits aren't genetic, your family likely played a role in forming yours."[3] She quotes Melissa Leong, money expert and author of *Happy Go Money*, "Money meaning grows on family trees. If money is something that is never discussed in the household, if it's seen as the root of evil, if it's a source of stress, those can leave a mark."[4]

Even if you don't feel like an expert in this area, your children are looking for direction. You might share what you've learned from good or not so good financial decisions in the past or about areas you're currently trying to manage better. Your lessons might just save your kids from having to learn from their own mistakes.

Perfectly Imperfect

We'll never be perfect in all these nine areas, nor will we nail any part of parenting perfectly all the time. But we can communicate to our kids that it's our heart's desire to honor God and model well for them. Confessing our mistakes, asking for forgiveness, and talking about the areas we're working on makes us more relatable and trustworthy to our kids. In fact, one of the worst things parents can do is act like they're never wrong, brushing off mistakes with excuses and being too proud to admit they made a mistake.

Confessing our mistakes, asking for forgiveness, and talking about the areas we're working on makes us more relatable and trustworthy to our kids.

While the points above may feel challenging, know that every parent who has cared about these things has felt the same way, including me. We may feel overwhelmed in the moment, but let's take heart knowing that caring enough to change is a beautiful step. Our window with these amazing kids is small, but our impact is huge!

This may be a good time to pray about some areas you want to work on. Your kids will thank you later—and Dr. Rick will be so proud.

A Word to Dads

We live on the North Shore of Oahu, charmingly known as "the country," and in some neighborhoods you'll find that the chickens outnumber the people. They frequently cross the street in front of me, sometimes dodging my car tires at the last second. On occasion I've seen a mother hen crossing the road with a whole line of chicks just in front of a car. As disaster is about to unfold, she'll make a sudden move to dodge out of the way, with just enough time for all her chicks to follow right behind with the same move. Thankfully, they're hardwired to stay right with the leader. It's part of what animal experts call the "imprinting process." Right from hatching out of the egg, chicks are drawn to their parent and wired to follow them wherever they go.

Your kids are the same way. How you respond to a particular situation, how you treat your wife and others around you, how you conduct every conversation you have in their presence . . . they're watching and listening and following right along and learning from your every move.

Day by day, you're teaching your sons what it is to be a husband, a father, a man. You're teaching your daughters what to look for in a man. Your kids will naturally follow you, just like those little chicks, for better or for worse. The recording button is always on—to capture the good, the bad, and the ugly. And if you're like me, you often forget that fact.

But then you're reminded of it each time your kids speak or act in a way you disapprove of, because as soon as you reprimand them, a little voice reminds you that you're guilty of the same thing. (Either the little voice in your head or the actual little one standing in front of you.)

I love to take credit when I catch my boys showing some form of discipline or patience that reflects what I've tried to live out or voicing some words of wisdom they've heard from me. At the same time, I have to admit that some of what's frustrated me in my boys' attitudes or actions can be traced back to me. Moments when I should have shown empathy or affection but didn't, times when I focused on facts and ignored feelings. It's subtle stuff sometimes, but I can see my own bad examples influencing my kids' hearts

Modeling life is a serious responsibility. I don't know about you, but I want to look back with as little regret as possible. At the same time, thank God for his grace in parenting in the areas we fail. That being said, I realize that our daily modeling at home may be one of the key ingredients in raising amazing kids.

Thoughts from Josiah, Age Twenty-Two

When I'm away at college and need to make a decision, thoughts of my dad often come up. Usually, it's when I'm in a moral dilemma, when I'm between a rock and a hard place. Other times I'm piecing together whether to say yes to yet another event or obligation. Still other times, I'm looking for help as a leader.

Whether it's because I have many memories of him treating people well and living with great integrity or it's simply because I've decided he's someone I don't mind turning out like, my dad comes to my mind quickly.

I often find myself asking the question, "What would Dad do?" Lately, I've realized that even when I lack the time to truly imagine what he would do, I end up making decisions much like the ones he would make or that I'd expect him to make if he were in my shoes. I know this is normal; it's how God wired us. Parents set the example for their kids. It's like they're setting the bar, or the standard, whether or not they realize it.

One day, as a parent, I'll remember my dad and the ways his behavior became either an excuse or a challenge for me. I'll remember that my job is not so much to tell my children how they should behave but to show them, to the best of my abilities, what a good life really looks like.

Reflection Questions

1. How much of my parenting is intentional, and how much might be patterns or habits I brought into my family from how I was raised?

2. What will my kids be like if they grow up to be just like me?

3. In what one area on the list above might I raise the bar for myself as I recognize that my kids are likely to model after me?

CHAPTER 4

THE VERY MOST IMPORTANT THING

Make Faith the Highest Priority

As soon as your children can understand
anything, let them know about Christ.
—Charles Spurgeon

This book is packed with what I'm most passionate about in parenting, but this chapter's content is the very best I have to offer. That's because my greatest advice for raising amazing kids is to introduce them to our most amazing God and then make him the most important part of your family life.

Nothing will make your kids more amazing than their having a personal relationship with the God who created them and loves them even more than you do. Not a character quality, not good grades, not sports achievement, not a dream job, not an ideal spouse, not a lifetime achievement award, or anything else. God's Spirit in our kids is as amazing as it gets.

Nothing will make your kids more amazing than their having a personal relationship with the God who created them and loves them even more than you do.

But want to hear a cool bonus? When our kids grow up to be Christ followers, they're likely to possess the other qualities we hope for as well! The way I see it, a young person committed to following God and living according to biblical principles will be more likely to make good choices. They'll have the resources and wisdom they need to navigate everything from relationships to health and lifestyle choices to work to money management and beyond. They won't be perfect (they're still human!), but they'll be growing to be more like Christ.

I'm convinced that if my kids grow up to be fully committed Christ followers, I have little to be concerned about. Really! Because if they grow up to have an authentic relationship with Jesus, they'll have wisdom to guide them, and they'll experience the most purpose-filled, peace-filled lives possible.

I'm not suggesting a struggle free or easy life but a life filled with the security of knowing they're loved and there's a purpose to their struggles. When we—and our kids—are on God's side, we get to walk through this life, with all its joys and challenges, alongside the King of Kings. Literally with the One who can see the end from the beginning. When we do life with God, we get to be a part of the most amazing adventure that's part of his cosmic story—a story that doesn't promise comfort or ease but is filled with truth and love and that most definitely guarantees a happy ending.

Can we just hang out on that thought for a minute? *That is about as amazing as it gets.*

So when it comes to faith, I vote we tell our kids the truth—the whole truth about the God who loves them and the journey that awaits them. Not a feel-good version or a made-up gospel that promises health and wealth, though. Because when our kids learn about the real Jesus—the one who laid down his life for their eternity, the One worthy of wonder and awe—and they understand that he's fully loving but also unbelievably powerful, it will be hard for them to resist the invitation to be part of his story.

Start Young!

Research tells us that most Christians become Christians during their childhood. It's much less likely for someone to make a commitment to Christ after they turn eighteen. Young children have precious, impressionable hearts, but as they grow up, things of the world creep in, and their hearts tend to harden. While there's always hope for anyone to begin a relationship with Jesus *at any age*, George Barna, renowned researcher, stated, "From the way I see it, our kids' faith is either won or lost by age 13."[1]

Time is of the essence. And, I will add, *your home is the best place to start.*

That's right. Before all this talk inspires you to hurry and sign your kids up for the next church event or Vacation Bible School, you need to know that research also tells us the best and most likely place for your kids to become Christians is at home—with you.

Other than God, no one loves your kids more than you do, and there's no one they look to or trust more than their parents, even if they don't show it. Your position in your child's life uniquely qualifies you to be the best ones to lead them into faith.

The best and most likely place for your kids to become Christians is at home—with you.

So, you might ask, how do we do that? Here are two ways to start.

Model Your Own Faith Walk

The number one thing you can do to inspire your kids to want an authentic relationship with God is to model your own authentic relationship with him. As we talked about in chapter 3, kids are watching and likely to model after all we do, and sooner or later they'll know if you're all talk or really believe what you're teaching.

Let me be clear. Nothing will impact your child's faith more than seeing you living out your own, genuine faith.

The stakes are high on this one. From the beginning, God gave parents the great privilege and responsibility of passing the baton of faith to their children. He commissioned his servant Moses to teach parents how to do this in the most intentional and authentic way in the book of Deuteronomy:

> You shall teach them diligently to your children, and shall talk of them when you sit in your house, and when you walk by the way, and when you lie down, and when you rise. You shall bind them as a sign on your hand, and they shall be as frontlets between your eyes. You shall write them on the doorposts of your house and on your gates. (Deuteronomy 6:7–9 ESV)

This is a picture of a lifestyle of genuine faith. Not of a "religious family" or a family that merely attends church. Instead, we see parents who "diligently teach" their kids about God and his Word, and then, well, talk about it a lot!

This topic is so near to my heart, because as my college boys visit for summer breaks or holidays, one of my favorite observations is how much they truly love to talk about Scripture. Around the dinner table or as we take family walks or hang out at the beach, it seems to never fail that someone will bring up a Bible topic from a recent sermon, podcast, or devotional time. And before you know it, we're all deep in a great conversation about God's Word.

But here's the thing: this isn't new. It didn't start in college. It all started when my kids were young. With Dad and Mom including Scripture in their days and with Bible stories. Dad would tuck the boys in bed at night and practice one simple verse with them until they had it memorized. As they grew up, our kids had daily devotions and later got involved in small group Bible studies with their youth leaders at church.

This is a lot of Bible, and for good reason: our kids need a whole lot of God's truth if we want any chance of counteracting the lies and darkness that will bombard them in this world. We desperately need God's Word to sustain our faith.

Jesus said, "Man shall not live on bread alone, but on every word that comes from the mouth of God" (Matt. 4:4). Dave and I know how much we need God's Word, so we've tried to set this as a normal, daily part of our family life.

Communicate the Gospel Clearly

Though the most important part of raising kids to know and love God is to live out your own faith authentically, it's still essential that you communicate the gospel message to them clearly. The gospel quite simply means "good news." It is the story of God demonstrating his love for us by sending his own Son to rescue us from our sins. Kids need to know that this one truth holds the key to their everything that matters, now and forever.

POP QUIZ

If you had to communicate the gospel message to someone right now in under two minutes, could you do it? Go ahead and practice, I'll wait . . .

So how'd you do?

If you didn't do so well, no worries! I'd love to help you get comfortable doing it. The cool thing about the gospel message is that it's so profound that theologians say we've still barely scratched the surface of it, yet it's also simple enough for a child to understand!

Dave and I try to communicate God's love to our kids as simply and often as we can. It's taken me some practice, but it can be fun to learn and pass on to your kids.

AN ACTUAL RECENT CONVERSATION BETWEEN LEVI AND ME

Me: "Levi, what if one of your friends asked you what it means to be a Christian?"

Levi: [slight groan but also a smile] "Mom, we've done this a thousand times!"

Me: "I know! But it's fun, right? [*wink*] Go ahead! What would you say?"

Levi: "I'd first tell them the Bible says God loves everyone."

Me: "Do you have a verse for that?"

Levi: "Can you just let me finish?"

Me: "Sorry."

Levi: "John 3:16 says, 'For God so loved the world that he gave his only Son, that whoever believes in him should not perish but have eternal life.'"

Me: "Awesome. Go on."

Levi: "Next, I'd tell them we're all sinners. That's Romans . . . um . . ."

Me: "It's 3:23."

Levi: "Mom! Romans 3:23: 'For all have sinned and fall short of the glory of God.'"

Me: "Yes! Then what?"

Levi: "Then I'd say that because we're sinners, we all deserve death (Romans 6:23) but that God sent his Son, Jesus, to die on the cross for us. Then he rose to heaven and promised to come back and take us to heaven with him if we will accept his gift."

Me: "Awesome. You're almost there. That means we need to . . ."

Levi: "We need to confess with our mouth that Jesus is Lord and believe in our heart that God raised him from the dead. If you do that you will be saved" (Romans 10:9).

Me: [High five and a big hug]

So, yes, in our family we have gone over this a few times (maybe not a thousand, but . . .) so Levi not only knows it but can share it with a friend if he has the opportunity. Of course, his personal understanding and ability to articulate it will grow as he grows, but this is a solid start.

Your family may use different words or Scriptures to share the gospel, so make it your own and natural for you and for the situation and person you're sharing with. And, of course, help your child with what they can understand at their stage of life.

Dave and I didn't want to assume our kids understood the gospel. We talk about it, and we talk about it being the most important thing they can ever embrace or share with someone. Then we make it conversational so that's exactly how they see it. Kids learn quickly, and repetition is key!

If you're new to the Bible or Christianity, don't be intimidated! God is inviting you into relationship too, and many resources are available to help you grow right alongside your child. In the resource section in the back of this book, you'll find a link to a simple download with the gospel message, complete with

Scriptures as well as simple steps to lead your child or a friend or yourself into a relationship with God. I hope it's helpful!

Your personal growth will inspire your child more than you might think, so don't be shy about sharing it.

Results ~~Guaranteed~~ Likely

When I talk about raising up kids to know and love God, the topic of "formula" never fails to come up. Most of us would love it if doing A and B might guarantee C. I get that. When it comes to our spiritual lives, however, it's not quite so simple. God has given us all a free will, and even if we teach our kids the gospel message and do everything we can to lead them to faith, they still might choose to turn away from God for a season—or for a lifetime. This is a painful reality, and one for which I don't have an easy answer.

I will never claim that introducing your kids to God and making him the center of your family life guarantees they'll love and follow him. There simply are no promises on outcome. A quick look at the Bible reminds us that many people God loved didn't respond accordingly but instead rebelled and rejected him. One of Jesus's own disciples betrayed him for a mere thirty silver coins!

Here is what I do know: not having a guaranteed outcome does not give us an excuse to sit back, hoping for the best, or to dish out our spiritual responsibilities to a church, school, or chance. There may not be a formula for parenting, but there certainly is a high calling to teach our kids diligently, to discipline fairly, and to live a godly life ourselves. We do what we can do, then we let God do what only God can do.

Tony Evans wrote, "The single greatest reason why we are losing our young people today is that the home is no longer the place where faith is transferred. Parents, the primary purpose of the home is the evangelization and discipleship of your children. You cannot outsource this vital component in the rearing of your children."[2]

Teaching your kids God's Word and making spiritual disciplines a normal, healthy (enjoyable!) part of your family life may not guarantee results, but it will greatly increase the chance that your children will grow up to make their faith their own.

Spiritual Disciplines Matter in Childhood

A study by Lifeway Research offers some encouraging data along these lines. Surveying Christian parents who had adult children ages eighteen to thirty, the study set out to determine which parenting practices pay off over the long haul when it comes to spiritual health.[3] In other words, which spiritual disciplines in childhood might predict the best spiritual condition when these kids grow into adulthood.

After years of research looking at thousands of families, their data showed strong correlations between childhood disciplines and adults who continued to embrace a vibrant faith. At the top of the list? Reading the Bible. Children who read the Bible regularly had the greatest likelihood of growing up to continue in a personal relationship with God.

I love what Jana Magruder, director of Lifeway Kids, concluded: "The key takeaway from the study is a simple yet profound finding that God's Word truly is what changes lives."[4]

In addition to reading the Bible, other childhood practices that predict spiritual health as adults include regular prayer time, attending church, listening primarily to Christian music, and participating in a church mission trip while growing up. Doing all five of these practices in childhood placed the young adults in the study above the 90th percentile!

Relationship > Religion

While we're talking about spiritual practices, I think it's important to note that these disciplines are part of a healthy relationship with God but *not* the end goal. Checking items off a list won't transform a child's heart. Only Christ can do that.

As kids grow up, it's more and more important for them to understand their relationship with Jesus and not confuse it with religious activities.

As kids grow up, it's more and more important for them to understand their relationship with Jesus and not confuse it with religious activities. Jesus was extremely hard on the Pharisees, who religiously followed hundreds of rules each day but missed the heart of God in what they did.

In Matthew 23:27, Jesus says, "Woe to you, teachers of the law and Pharisees, you hypocrites! You are like whitewashed tombs, which look beautiful on the outside but on the inside are full of the bones of the dead and everything unclean."

I'm a big fan of the local church, and the Bible makes it clear that we're meant to live out our faith lives in community (Hebrews 10:25). But we don't want to look to churchy things in place of a personal relationship with God.

It's also worth noting that many people have been hurt by religious groups or churches, and I understand some of you may have chosen to steer clear of organized religion because of that. I'm sorry if religion has put a bad taste in your mouth. But I want to encourage you to reconsider. Rather than give up on church, I suggest you try again! Seek out a healthy, Christ-centered church to get involved with. You won't find perfect people at any church, but if our perfect God is at the center, you're in good company. And the blessings outweigh the human factor if you go in with a humble and receptive heart.

Faith as Kids Grow Up

Young kids are often eager learners and happy to curl up on Mom or Dad's lap to listen to Bible stories. But then they grow up. They spend time with other people. They learn about other values and spiritual practices and discover more of what the world has to offer. They also have a sin nature that's growing right alongside—or should I say *inside*—them.

Sadly, some parents don't recognize this is happening. In the busyness of life, they don't pick up on clues that their child is drifting away from the faith they've been taught. Other parents anticipate this coming and might be tempted to, well, freak out. I get plenty of emails with questions and concerns like these:

- What do I do when my kids question the faith we've taught them?
- What can we do to protect our kids from the world and its antagonism toward the Christian faith?
- If I force my children to read the Bible or go to church, I'm afraid it will make them rebel.

The first thing I'm going to say (maybe even shout—in the kindest way, of course,) is this: *Do not ignore it when you see your child drifting from the faith.*

Also, please don't assume your teenager believes in what you taught them in their childhood. The teen years are when all the things you taught your children when they were younger can be put into practice and developed. These are the years when their faith can not only become personal but vibrant and meaningful. But they're also the years when their faith will be challenged—sometimes greatly so. Your kids need you more than ever during this season. Your role will change, yes, but they still need you as they grow up to own their own faith.

Here are my three suggestions for spiritual parenting as kids enter their teenage years:

1. Establish an Open Environment to Discuss Spiritual Matters

As our kids grow up, we need to anticipate and welcome conversations about spiritual topics. Don't be afraid of doubts; welcome them! My husband has always said, "Doubts are the seeds of faith," because he's personally taken his own questions and doubts to the Word of God and found it to prove itself as true and trustworthy.

We often walked our kids through their questions, finding answers in Scriptures to help them sort through topics that came up. From the validity of the creation to sexual purity, we looked to God's Word as our authority. As they got older, we challenged them to find answers in God's Word on their own—and then we could discuss it with them. We wanted them to be critical thinkers, able to discern truth from error.

2. Be Sure Your Teens Are Connected to Christian Mentors Beyond Mom and Dad

By the time kids are in middle and high school, they begin to need people beyond Mom and Dad to model an authentic relationship with God. Their parents will remain the number one influence in their kids' lives, yes, but these outside people will begin to play a new role. An important one.

My three older boys were all part of two church youth groups during their high school years, and eventually they got involved in small group Bible studies. These involvements became a huge point of growth and mentorship for them.

Sometimes when one of our sons was trying to make a decision or work through a hard season, instead of getting involved we suggested he bring it up with his youth group leader. This set a pattern for his future years when we wouldn't always be nearby, hoping he would find trustworthy mentors to connect with.

The smaller groups our boys met with also provided them with accountability related to the temptations teenagers face. They had leaders who asked hard questions and challenged them to stand strong in their convictions.

3. Don't Give Up the Spiritual Disciplines

There's no doubt that kids need to develop more independence as they grow up, but we should be guiding that process. Dave and I believe there should still be rules, requirements, and expectations as long as our children are under eighteen and living at home. We've made it a normal expectation that they'll read their Bibles daily, gather with the family for occasional devotions or times of worship and prayer, and go to church regularly, which sometimes means requesting Sundays off from a job. Attending a church with other young people your kids enjoy seeing is helpful here!

These disciplines aren't a "have to" but a "get to" in our family. We talk about them as a joy and a privilege. Our boys all love church, and Sundays are usually the most social times of our week. Because of that, so far, our kids haven't resisted going. Nor have they resisted any of the above disciplines.

Kids feel most secure when their parents establish firm requirements and boundaries for them. Teenagers are prone to laziness (aren't we all?), and if given the chance to skip just about any discipline, they often will. So I recommend being purposeful about where you offer them freedom and where you hold the line.

The Battle Is Real

This conversation about raising kids to know and love God would be incomplete without specifically mentioning the spiritual battle that is described in Scripture and experienced every day in our real life, whether we recognize it or not. In 1 Peter 5:8 we are warned to "be alert and of sober mind. Your enemy the devil prowls around like a roaring lion looking for someone to devour." In 2 Corinthians 10:4 we read that "the weapons we fight with are not the weapons of the world." Though the topics we have covered in this chapter will equip a child to stand in faith against the enemy's schemes, a deeper understanding of the spiritual battle that exists and the armor available to us (see Ephesians 6:10–11) will be helpful for parents and kids alike. Because this topic is so important, I wrote a bonus chapter called "Amazing Armor: Preparing your Kids to Face Spiritual Battles." Find a link to it in the resource section.

The Greatest Joy

The Bible verse that most inspires my parenting is 3 John 1:4: "I have no greater joy than to hear that my children are walking in the truth." As my boys are growing into young adults, I resonate so deeply with that verse. I'm convinced that making our kids' relationship with God our greatest parenting priority will not only offer them the best life but bring us the most joy as parents.

I'm praying for you, parents, and I hope that you, too, have the chance to experience that same joy.

A Word to Dads

Dads, as we've already touched on in the previous chapters, how you live out your faith and express it obviously matters. It's the essence of your own relationship with God. But less obvious, at times, is that it matters to your children and for generations of your family to come. A lot hinges on your willingness to trust and believe God and his Word. Heavy stuff, I know. I guess this is part of working out your own salvation with "fear and trembling" (Phil. 2:12).

Let's break it down a little.

First, your faith matters to God because he gave it to you (Eph. 2:8–9). It's the means by which you entered into and continue in your relationship with him. It's also the essence of living out what you believe and acknowledging to God what he's given you (Heb. 11:6). But what he gives to you must be put into practice. You live it out. The Bible is full of people who did just that and did it well, leaving an amazing legacy for us to admire and follow (see the "Hall of Faith" in Hebrews 11:4–39).

In the New Testament, Paul gave his young disciple Timothy some advice in this area of living out faith. He talked about fanning his faith into flame (2 Tim. 1:6). A flame can be seen and felt more and more the brighter it gets. It goes from being unseen in the heart to being seen and lived out in the body. Our faith shows.

And how you live it out affects the faith of those around you, specifically your kids. God's Word suggests that, in his sovereign and divine plan, he intends to put into effect something like a faith transfer from one generation to another. It's implied in Paul's description of the origins of young Timothy's aforementioned faith that "first lived" in his grandmother Lois and in his mother Eunice. Similarly, as Monica mentioned, one of our favorite passages, Deuteronomy 6:7–9, was sort of a how-to for the Israelite parents in passing the faith on to their children. It was up to the fathers to "impress" these things on their children. We also see this plan echoed in the words of Psalm 78: "He commanded our fathers to teach to their children, that the next generation might know them [God's law], the children yet unborn, and arise and tell them to their children, so that they should set their hope in God and not forget the works of God, but keep his commandments" (vv. 5–7 ESV). Conversely, in the New Testament, in Mark 9:42, Jesus gives an unsettling warning that seems to be directed at adults who would dare to intentionally lead children away from God and his word. Something worse than being thrown into the sea with a millstone around one's neck makes it clear that God cares about what we teach our children. Our parenting behavior and decision-making have eternal consequences.

In the end, the formation of your kid's faith, by God's grace, may not involve you, but as we've read, the blueprint given in the Bible suggests that it should!

Dads, how are you doing with this stuff? Do your kids know what it's like to see their father depending on God? Are you honest with them about your need for the Savior? Do they hear you voicing your thoughts and ideas about what God has revealed to you about life and the things that matter? Do they have a dad who's carving out time for daily devotions? Do they get to hear you verbalize your responses to the tough questions the world is throwing at them to challenge a faith in God? Are they equipped with answers you've provided them from God's Word?

At a more basic level, do they know how to pray and read God's Word through the example you're giving them? Do they know they have an earthly father whose greatest desire is for his children to know their heavenly Father?

Dads, I hope you take time to consider and to keep reminding yourself how critical it is to live out your faith and pass it on to your daughters and sons. In light of eternity, nothing is more important to your family!

Thoughts from Luke, Age Eighteen

I've always known faith to be a natural part of life, though from a young age I understood that not everyone shares my family's Christian beliefs. I remember being at the skatepark as a seven- or eight-year-old, often casually asking kids if they "knew Jesus." I'm sure at times this question came across a bit out of left field and maybe seemed strange, but I never felt that way.

After all, I knew Jesus and understood how important he is, so I didn't see why they shouldn't too. I'd seen my parents and older brothers talk to people about Jesus, and even though I didn't really know the best way to do it, I wanted to do the same. Of course, with age came maturity and also social awareness, and I've gained some wisdom in how I talk to strangers about my faith. That's not to say, however, that the boldness and weight

I put on these matters were misplaced. I hope to always approach the world in which I live with that same kind of childlike faith.

Although my faith has always been my own, I'm grateful for the example of my parents and my brothers and their faith throughout my growing up years. It was so important, and it still is today. It's quite amazing to think back to all the ways they indirectly encouraged me through their constant reliance on God.

Now I spend much of my time traveling for surf contests. Most of the time I'm with other people, and rarely are they Christians. During these times I've been so grateful for that foundation of faith I share with everyone at home. *My parents taught me at a young age that true faith doesn't disappear when the crowd changes or when I'm away from home.* True faith puts God first no matter where I am or what I'm doing.

While traveling, however, you often encounter experiences that test faith. Whether it's peer pressure or having freedom to do whatever you want, you're in a position to make decisions. These times are when I find my true, foundational strength in my faith. I'm so grateful for the good times and the hard times when I travel, though, because I know God is right there with me, and I can always rely on him for my strength.

I believe strong faith means following God even when it's hard or no one is around to tell you what to do, but I also know my parents care when they check in and ask me if I'm staying on top of reading my Bible and spending time in prayer. Of all the gifts they've given me, a relationship with God is the very most important.

Reflection Questions

1. Are you able to communicate your own faith story
    (your "testimony") and the basic gospel message
    to your kids and others? If not, what steps might
    you take to be able to talk about these things
    comfortably?

2. Which spiritual discipline do you need to work on
    most with your kids? Bible reading? Prayer? Being
    in church and fellowship with others? Serving?

3. What outside mentors are you pointing your kids
    toward to help them grow? If you don't yet have a
    "village" of spiritual influences in your kids' lives,
    where might you look to find some?

CHAPTER 5

FOCUS ON THE FOUNDATION

Give the Gift of a Healthy Marriage

> *We do not develop habits of genuine love*
> *automatically. We learn them by watching*
> *effective role models—most specifically by*
> *observing how our parents express love for each*
> *other day in and day out.*
> —Josh McDowell

The Swansons are big fans of *The Incredibles*, and I have a favorite scene from the original film. When Bob and Helen Parr, also known as Mr. Incredible and Elastigirl, are away facing their greatest rival, their kids are left behind, and the tensions rise. Trying to alert her brother to the extent of danger their parents are facing, Violet says my favorite lines: "What do you think is going on here? You think we're on vacation or something? Mom and Dad's lives could be in jeopardy. Or worse, their marriage!"

Hollywood pleasantly surprises me sometimes. Even Violet, the shy, sulky teenage daughter, understands that a threat to their parents' marriage would be about as bad as it gets.

The health of their parents' marriage deeply impacts a child's sense of security. When I was in fourth grade, I distinctly remember becoming aware of the concept of divorce. A few of my friends' parents were divorcing, and fear crept over me as I wondered if there was any chance my parents could get divorced too.

While I'm grateful that my fear was unfounded, you may know that feeling in a more personal way. Perhaps you're the child of divorced parents, and if you were old enough at the time to remember now, I'd guess you have distinct memories of the moment you realized your family was being divided.

As it turned out, my parents weren't only committed to their marriage for a lifetime, but I was soon to learn that the "D" word was off limits in my family. While goofing around with my brothers one day, one of us joked that "Mom and Dad could get divorced!" in earshot of my dad. We made that mistake only once. I'll never forget my dad's face as he let us kids know, in no uncertain terms, that the "D" word would never be spoken regarding the two of them again. It was a firm rebuke, but deep down it made me feel incredibly secure.

Dave and I were both raised by parents who were committed to their marriage for a lifetime, and we know that's rare today. We're fully aware of the gift our folks have given us in that legacy.

Since I realize this isn't the norm, let me pause right here and remind you that you had zero control over your own parents' marital status. That was outside of your control. But the great news is that you do have full control of the legacy you pass on to your own children. Even if you're divorced or are raising children on your own, the messages about marriage you give your kids can dramatically influence their security and future choices.

Marriage, between one man and one woman for a lifetime, was God's idea, and I believe that honoring and protecting that covenant plays a great role in raising amazing kids.

I'll share a few suggestions for divorced/single parents at the end of this chapter. You can still make an incredible impact on how your kids think about marriage!

Tend to Your Marriage

First, marriage is hard.

In his book *Habits of the Household*, Justin Whitmel Earley wrote, "Marriage is radical because Christianity is radical, and that is a beautiful thing to display to our children. It's a nod to the God who has loved us into loving. When we rehearse the covenant of marriage in front of them, we rehearse the promise of our own salvation in front of them: God is a God who never gives up on love, so neither will we."[1]

And growing a *healthy* marriage is hard. Twenty-six years in, I would say Dave and I have the healthiest marriage we've ever had. Yet two days ago we got into an ugly argument during the twenty minutes our kids went to the grocery store after dinner. I wish that wasn't true, but it is. We're sinners, saved by grace, and our marriage reminds us of our daily need for grace.

The devil has a target on my marriage—and yours. Again, marriage was God's idea, and the Enemy has hated it from the beginning. He introduced the blame game right from the get-go between Adam and Eve, and he's targeted husbands and wives ever since. If he can take you down via your relationship with your spouse, then his job is easy. The wreckage will be great. A single broken marriage affects generations.

If we expect these attacks, we're able to go into marriage challenges with eyes wide open. If we know the landmines are out there, we'll be a lot less likely to step on one. Marriage, it turns out, has a lot to do with God refining us individually, and it has the potential of reflecting his covenant love to our children in a special way. We want our kids to see, firsthand, that loving our spouse

We want our kids to see, firsthand, that loving our spouse well may not be easy, but it's good and godly work.

well may not be easy, but it's good and godly work. We have the best opportunity to show our kids that in marriage, even when it's hard, we don't give up.

Vows

As I write, our family is grieving the passing of Dave's mom. She was eighty-six years old and lived a wonderful life that honored God. Five years ago she was diagnosed with Alzheimer's disease, and in a short time she lost her memory, her ability to communicate, and, sadly, a whole lot of her dignity. Alzheimer's is not a kind disease; however, one of the few silver linings from this turn of events was observing my father-in-law's response.

Dave's parents had always been traditional in their roles—his dad worked hard as a scientist and businessman, and his mom worked hard as a full-time homemaker. Karin did all the cooking and cleaning, paid bills, organized the family schedule, and served her community tirelessly. She made a beautiful home for Dave's dad, Lyn, to return to each evening. Greeting him with a kiss at the doorway and usually dinner on the table, she made June Cleaver look basic. (And if you don't know who June Cleaver is, thanks for making me feel old.)

Before Karin's health began to decline, she and Lyn moved from their home in the country into a retirement community where they lived independently but with many options for assisted living care as needed. Their home was located across the street from an Alzheimer's care building, which Lyn could transfer Karin to at any point. No one would have faulted Lyn, who was still healthy and sharp, for placing Karin where she would have full-time care so he might have the chance to enjoy some freedom during his retirement.

Yet Lyn chose to keep Karin home, being her full-time caregiver until the end when someone helped part-time. We knew how much work this was for Lyn, who suddenly had to manage all home responsibilities, feed and bathe his wife, and care for her much like he would care for a child. When Dave's aunt reminded Lyn that he had care options, he quietly, humbly replied, "I made a vow."

My father-in-law's dedicating sixty-six years of marriage to one woman and then caring for her in sickness, not *just* in health, till death parted them may have been one of the greatest parenting examples he set for those of us coming up after him.

This is a difficult topic to approach as I'm aware that a good number of parents reading this have already divorced or may be facing that reality now. I imagine not one of you thought that would be your story, and many of you didn't choose it. You may believe in vows with all your heart and wish you could change your circumstances.

But we live in a fallen world, and marriage is one of the common casualties. I don't want to communicate shame or discourage any of you. Instead, I hope to offer some encouragement for those of you who are married and perhaps inspire perspective for those who are not.

For those of you who are married, I want to bring both a strong word of encouragement and caution. Your marriage is incredibly important, and I can't overemphasize how crucial it is that you tend to it carefully. In every season. You should not allow your kids to become the center of the family or let them or anything else get between you and your spouse.

Next to modeling a genuine relationship with Jesus, a strong and healthy marriage is the greatest gift you can give your kids. Research has shown that children being raised by parents married to each other tend to be healthier (mentally, emotionally, and physically), do better in school, and make better life choices than children who are not being raised within marriage.[2] Guard your marriage as though your life depends on it.

> *Next to modeling a genuine relationship with Jesus, a strong and healthy marriage is the greatest gift you can give your kids.*

Divorce is not an unpardonable sin, and God allows for divorce in certain situations. I know single parents, divorced or widowed, who are working hard to raise amazing children, and I'm wholly convinced it can be done. It just won't be easy.

If you are married, however, making your marriage a high priority, before kids and work and outside interests, is one of the most crucial choices you can make to bless your children.

Following are some of my best tips for cultivating your marriage in all seasons, gathered from wise mentors and more than twenty-six years of personal experience.

1. **Invest time into it.** Do this in all seasons. Make daily connections. Take walks and spend couch time together. Make phone calls or text. And treat your spouse like your best friend, both in public and in private.

2. **Pray together.** If you're not comfortable praying together, break through that. You might start with a book of prayers for your family and read the prayers all together.

I also recommend just the two of you pray a quick prayer together each morning or night, but even a weekly routine is a great start.

3. **Play together.** Remember falling in love. Go back to doing some of the things you did then. I know you're busy, but it's worth it. And don't wait for your spouse to initiate fun and laughter. You can do it.

4. **Nurture your sex life.** Sex, like marriage, was God's idea, and it connects husband and wife in a way nothing else can. Sex is good for your health and releases chemicals that bond you together in a mysterious and profound way. If this is a difficult area for you, get help. Books, counselors, and plenty of other resources are available.

5. **Talk to someone when you need help.** Marriage counselors and therapists can play a great role in helping work out issues, big or small. Dave and I have been blessed through marriage counseling, and early on in our marriage, we reached out to older couples we respected to share some of our struggles and ask for wisdom. This was scary to initiate, but when couples we looked up to told us they'd been where we were, we felt far less alone.

6. **Take God's idea of "leaving and cleaving" seriously.** Once you're married, you must cut the childhood (and any childish) ties with your family of origin. Hopefully, you can maintain a great relationship with them, but your identity and security are now tied to your spouse.

7. **Minister together.** Serve the poor. Volunteer in Sunday school. Lead (or at least be involved in) small group Bible studies. Serving alongside your spouse will knit you together.

8. **Value teamwork.** Husbands and wives were made to help and complement each other. Mutual respect will be

reflected in how you support and encourage the other. Consider your spouse your teammate and speak words that reflect that—both to them and behind their back!

9. **Have a regular date night.** Intentionally set aside time to connect, nurture your marriage, and enjoy each other's company. And protect that time. What you do doesn't have to be fancy or expensive. A candlelight dinner on the porch with kids tucked in early counts. Note: Find a download with ten amazing date night ideas in the resource section.

10. **Get away together.** Extravagant vacations may not be feasible financially or logistically, but if you plan and save, you can at least spend a few simple days away each year. Consider a staycation at a local hotel, camping, or a day trip. Make it a priority. Side benefit: the dreaming and planning are part of the fun!

11. **Flirt.** Once again, remember what you did at first, and then do more of it. If your spouse isn't the type to initiate flirtation, it's OK for you to do it. (I do!) Texting is great for that, but using code is wise in case little eyes might sneak a look at your phone. Also, double-check your contacts. You wouldn't want to accidentally send your flirtatious text to *Dave the plumber.*

12. **Guard against temptation.** Stay away from situations that could open you up to emotional or sexual temptation. Place filters on your devices and welcome accountability for anything that's been an issue for you in the past. Setting up guardrails like choosing to never be alone with someone of the opposite sex other than your spouse may seem cumbersome, but it will be well worth it in the long run. Also, what a great example to your kids! With this I will mention guarding your heart by refusing to compare your spouse or your relationship with those of others.

Comparison is said to be the thief of joy, and there is no doubt comparison can steal your joy in marriage.

13. **Ask for forgiveness.** Friends, we need to humble ourselves daily. This can be extremely difficult in marriage, but it does get easier the more you make it normal. Robert Quillen said, "A happy marriage is the union of two good forgivers."[3]

14. **Serve each other.** Once again, this is a learned skill that can make a radical difference in your marriage. Don't wait for your spouse to serve you; look for ways to serve your spouse. This most often inspires a reciprocal action, but even if it doesn't, you're doing the right thing.

15. **Grow individually and together.** Keep trying to be an interesting partner. Seek to embrace a growth mentality. And don't let yourself go physically. Women, you don't have to look like a supermodel, but taking care of yourself physically is going to be good for you and your marriage. And, men, the dadbod is funny, but we actually appreciate it when you take care of yourself. We should all be constantly trying to take care of and even improve ourselves, and doing it together is the best way, especially if you hope to grow old (feeling good!) together.

We have such an incredible opportunity to show our kids God's unrelenting, self-sacrificing love as we walk out love in our marriage. Again, it won't be easy, but it will be beautiful. And one thing I know from experience (and from some wise people) is that marriage only grows richer with time. Keep pressing on, my friends. Pray for your marriage, invest in your marriage, and fight for your marriage. Let God's love lead you.

Single parents, here are a few suggestions for helping your children develop a positive attitude toward marriage:

- Look for opportunities to speak well of marriage, point out people who seem to have happy, loving marriages, and encourage your kids to anticipate a healthy marriage in their future.
- If divorce is part of your story, plan how you want to communicate about your marriage and specifically about your children's other parent. *And stick with it.* You can be honest while not dragging out your former spouse's dirty laundry or speaking ill of your ex. Avoid topics unnecessary for your children to hear. They should not be a sounding board for your frustrations. Try to set aside personal pain (and pride) for the greater good of giving your children a positive association with marriage. Own your own mistakes and talk about what you've learned, as is age appropriate.
- Teach your kids about God's design for marriage. Help them understand that a good marriage will always take work, and that there's no such thing as a perfect marriage.

A Word to Dads

Hey, dads. Seeing your children blossom into the amazing humans they were created to be involves a number of important ingredients. But the ingredient that stands out above the rest is your marriage. It's the bedrock of the family and lays the foundation we can stand on to tackle all the issues on the road to raising amazing kids.

With so many marriages ending in divorce, too many dads have given up and abandoned ship. Sadly, many moms are left trying to fill all or some of Dad's roles. The gaps in parenting are being filled by other entities, social programs constructed by a system that doesn't value and can't be a replacement for the unique role a dad who's committed to a wife in marriage can.

Your kids need a secure and stable place to grow. They need a mom and dad who together provide unique masculine and feminine qualities that, when they're married, weave tightly together to create a home to grow up in. Your relationship with your wife is an anchor. With all the uncertainty in the world, your kids need to know that Mom and Dad are certain. They need to know they can count on you to be there and to be there together.

Your marriage allows the two of you to work together on meeting your kids' unique needs that will arise over time. You're able to be a tag team and problem-solve as issues come up in your children's lives. Two heads are better than one, and each of you comes at situations with a unique angle tied to your personality and gender. Sometimes children need the tender nurturing that only Mom can give, and other times they need a version of strength and discipline that's unique to Dad.

Your kids also just need to see a dad and mom living out a loving marriage relationship. Through the highs and lows, ups and downs, they need to see how two loving people work things out. You have an opportunity to give your kids what they need by being loyal, faithful, and self-sacrificial in your marriage.

I know this may be one of the hardest things you do in your life, especially if you're going through difficult times in your marriage relationship, but don't quit! Whatever you do, don't think that ending your marriage will make life easier, because it usually won't. Do the work. Invest the time. Be patient. Realize that God created marriage, and he did it to complete his creation plan. He created it for you. He created it for your wife. He created it for your children. It's sacred. So guard and take care of it more than anything else on this earth!

Thoughts from Jonah, Age Twenty

"Date night!" my mom would periodically announce to the family as far back as I can remember. Whenever I heard this, I always got excited, because that meant my brothers and I had a whole night at home to do something fun without the supervision of our parents. Hurray! ("Bro night!" my little brother Levi has labeled these nights.)

Looking back on these date nights, though, I can see they illustrated something important about my parents' relationship: *they are a team.* I thought date nights were kind of cheesy, yet it's striking that the whole idea of a date night is to intentionally set aside time to share with someone you love. This isn't easy when people are busy, irritable, and stressed.

But whenever my parents spent time together, worked together, complimented each other, or even just ran errands together, I knew they loved each other. When my mom spent intentional time with my dad talking and being his best friend, I knew they truly cared for each other. They set an example of what marriage should look like. Rather than letting two conflicting interests dominate each of their lives, my parents had a marriage that looked like a partnership, involving both members "dying" to themselves so they could best serve the family together.

I have a much clearer picture of harmonious marriage because of how my parents served each other and in so doing served our whole family. I hope my future marriage will resemble my parents' marriage and that my family will never use the "D" word so long as we live.

Reflection Questions

1. When you reflect on your marriage, where can you see the Enemy targeting your relationship?

2. Which tip for tending to your marriage seems most needed currently?

3. What's one way you might give your kids the gift of security in communicating about your marriage (or their future marriage)?

CHAPTER 6

THE SECRET WEAPON OR THE GREATEST DANGER

Understand the Power of Influences

> The conscience of children is formed by the
> influences that surround them; their notions
> of good and evil are the result of the moral
> atmosphere they breathe.
>
> —Jean Paul

Laws govern our natural world—the laws of gravity, relativity, and inertia to name a few. Sometimes they work in your favor, like when gravity allows you to go for a walk without floating out into the atmosphere. Other times gravity is a bummer, like when you drop your brand-new cell phone on a gravel road. (Speaking from experience here.)

When it comes to our human nature, we must also live by certain laws to experience a good life, like it or not. The book of Proverbs offers many principles for living well, which if heeded can help us make wise choices and avoid the relational equivalents to those phone-on-gravel moments. Dave and I are big fans of the book of Proverbs and have our teenage boys read a chapter a day. A few "laws" of human nature on the topic of influence have been especially helpful as we have raised our sons:

> Whoever keeps company with the wise
>> becomes wise,
>> but the companion of fools suffers harm.
>> (Prov. 13:20 ISV)

> Don't hang out with angry people;
>> don't keep company with hotheads.
> Bad temper is contagious—
>> don't get infected. (Prov. 22:24–25 MSG)

> As iron sharpens iron,
>> so a friend sharpens a friend. (Prov.
>> 27:17 NLT)

The principle of influence—just like the influence of the laws of nature—is not up for debate. It's part of our human nature.

Here's good news for parents: If you tap into the power of good influences in your children's lives when they're young, you'll discover a key to raising amazing kids. Good influences can be a secret weapon for good: by surrounding young kids with excellent influences—in books and media, music, friends, and role models—you can make your job a billion times easier. Good influences act as a "team," calling your child up to an excellent life.

But there may be no faster way to take a child down than the power of a bad influence. Most of us can recall some bad influences in our lives that left us with hard lessons learned.

Staying on top of the influences in your kid's life can be a big job for several reasons. First, to some degree those influences are hard to predict and may to some extent be outside your control. (I'm looking at you, neighborhood kids, classmates, and team-mates.) Weekends at a dad or mom or grandparent's house where rules and supervision may be a world apart from what you choose in your home.

While some of you may be blessed to live in a neighborhood with the sweetest kids from excellent families who embrace godly values, let's be honest. That's rare. If your kids go to school outside your home, play sports, or join any kind of team or club—or heck, if they go to Sunday school or youth group—they're most likely to find themselves with some *iffy influences* in the mix.

Second, while we might be able to orchestrate our ideal pseudo-bubble of heavenly influences around our *young kids*, at some point they must grow up to know, live in, and navigate the real world out there. And as they gain independence, the influence equation will shift from being in your control to something they'll have to choose. Therefore, a great part of your job will be convincing your kids that choosing good, wholesome, godly influences is indeed in their best interest.

Last, staying on top of the influences in our kids' lives will no doubt cost us. I can recall countless times when it would have been *so . . . very . . . easy* to let one of my boys just go to the sleepover, or cruise in the neighborhood, or spend a day at the beach with the local crew. It would have given me a break, allowing Dave and me to have a date night (or overnight to ourselves!). I could have skipped yet another drive across the North Shore on a heavy traffic day.

Yet when I considered what my boys would likely be exposed to or influenced by in each situation, I had to make some hard choices between my ease and convenience (plus making my kids

A great part of your job will be convincing your kids that choosing good, wholesome, godly influences is indeed in their best interest.

temporarily happy) and what I knew would be best for them in the big picture.

In his book *Raising Kingdom Kids*, Tony Evans wrote, "Parents, raising kingdom kids comes with a high price tag of time, energy, investment, and many other things, but when you take your eyes off the cost and focus instead on the size of the legacy you are producing, you will realize that it's worth every single thing that you invest."[1]

Let's talk about some of the most important influences in our kids' lives and how we might handle them with care.

Family

In chapter 3, we already spent time talking about the significance of your influence, Mom and Dad (make sure you didn't miss that one!). The next influences in line are the other family members who play a role in your kids' lives, especially in the early years. And there's no doubt that this can get . . . tricky!

I'm a huge fan of family—siblings, grandparents, aunties, uncles, and cousins. I love them all! If a child is blessed to grow up spending solid time with a whole bunch of extended family, a lot of good can come from it. (And my boys would be envious!) I hope you carve out time to enjoy and bond with the family that's near you!

But not all our relatives share our values and convictions, and handling this may require a lot of discernment and tact. Most often, communicating your family rules about your convictions is effective. You might need to help Grandma and Grandpa understand your concerns over the kids' screen time or why you prefer they don't reward your toddler with candy. You might have to ask an aunt or uncle to work with you on a boundary you set out of personal conviction even if they don't share it.

Of course, we want to express appreciation for those helpful people in our kids' lives, and I've personally found areas where I can compromise a bit. (I'm OK if my boys get extra sugared cereal and cartoon time at Grandma and Grandpa's house, because I love the relationship they have, and it doesn't happen every day.) But sometimes the influence of a relative has a harmful or outright toxic effect on your family. Sad as it is, some situations call for us to limit our kids' exposure to these people—or even keep some distance for a season.

Research shows that in child sexual abuse cases, the abuser is often related to the victim.[2] With this in mind, it's important to make choices about our kids spending time with relatives based on wisdom, not just family relationship. You don't *have to* allow kids to sleep over with cousins just because they're cousins. You can—and should—set boundaries on your kids' time with anyone you don't feel 100 percent comfortable watching them. Your kids are your greatest responsibility, and the stories of childhood abuse and molestation by a family member are too many and tragic to ignore.

As much as I wish I didn't need to, I'll add here that you need to keep your parental radar up even for kids in your immediate family. If you have an inkling of concern that one of your children or stepchildren has been influenced by pornography or been sexually exploited, then I recommend you don't allow them to be alone with your younger children. Sadly, in this hyper-sexualized world we live in, pedophilia and other forms of sexual abuse are not uncommon. Learning that a teenager has been influenced by pornography would be difficult enough to deal with, and how much worse to learn that your younger child has been their victim. These are things that cannot be unseen or undone, and the repercussions of even a single incident can be tragic.

I just mentioned the worst-case scenarios, but we must not overlook the more subtle influences relatives can have on our kids with their language, attitude, and perspectives on life. These matter too! Never lose sight of the fact that your children will become like the company they keep.

Now that I've highlighted a whole lot of caution on this topic, I must circle back to the positive by reiterating the great gift extended family can be. I encourage you to lean into the sweet familiar and familial relationships unique to all others. Extended family can fill a need when parents have busy work schedules, offering to give kids rides or snacks or be a cheering section at an event.

Family relationships are also likely to be lifelong. Even if your kids grow up to go in different directions than their cousins do, when family members go through something difficult, like a sickness or death in the family, most of the time it's extended family who show up.

We should encourage our kids to get to know and appreciate their extended family, because they will always be a uniquely God-given gift in their lives.

Friendships

Friendship is such an important part of growing up. Most of us can recall some of our happiest childhood memories involving friendships. Yet most of us can also trace some of our greatest mistakes or regrets back to a friendship with someone who was a bad influence on us. How can we steer our kids toward healthy friendships and help them avoid bad influences?

I don't think any of us really want to raise our kids in a bubble (OK, maybe just a little), but that's not what we're talking about here. Helping your child navigate friendships is *not* being over-protective! Wise and responsible parents will steer their child away from influences they know will be negative in the early years, and they'll have honest conversations about friendships with older kids.

This doesn't mean we prohibit any relationship that's not ideal; in fact, we should want our children to interact socially with all kinds of kids through sports, school, or in other community-type activities. But we should help them choose the friends they'll be close to—spend the most time with and trust on a deeper level. Friends who will build them up and not tear them down.

We should teach our kids that a good friend will:

- Be kind and not hurtful or mean.
- Bring out their best.
- Never try to get them to break rules or disobey their parents.
- Inspire them to be a better person.
- Call them out if they're heading in a bad direction.

In the early years, fostering friendship is pretty simple for us parents. We often get to choose our children's friends based on the parents we want to hang out with. As long as kids can play together decently, everything is typically cool. But then as kids grow up and gain some independent thought, they also form opinions on who they do and do not want to spend time with. If we've already opened conversations about both what to look for in a friend and how to be a good friend, we're off to a great start.

The next step is to keep the conversation going, asking questions and coaching our kids along as they grow up.

In my book *Boy Mom*, I wrote about my older boys going through some lonely years as teenagers. I heard from many readers who resonated with that, so I'll briefly share our experience again here.

In their early teen years, some of my sons' closest childhood friends started making bad decisions and getting into trouble, which isn't unusual in the early high school years. No longer wanting to be involved with those kids led to a lonely season for my boys. (Keep in mind we live in a small community.) But then one of the boys really wanted to "try" hanging out with a crew of young teens I knew were mostly unsupervised and getting into trouble. He was bored and lonely, and he argued that he could hang out with them without their being a bad influence on him.

He might as well have told me gravity doesn't apply to him. *It does. And they will.*

I empathized with my son, and we had some good chats about the situation. I suggested he invite some of the kids over to our house, individually, where he might have the chance to get to know them and perhaps be a good influence. But at that point it was much cooler for them to hang out as a group, so sadly, over time these "friends" quit responding to his invitations.

My boys kept going to youth group at church and seeing other kids when they surfed or skated at the skatepark, but for a season they often felt left out or alone. We prayed for new friends and helped them keep busy exploring hobbies and being involved in the youth group while also trying to come up with fun things to do as a family.

Time passed, and by their last year of high school, each of them had developed some new friends. Not necessarily in the "cool" crew, but good friends nonetheless. They also spent a lot of time with their youth leaders, who shared some of the same recreational interests our boys had. We kept pointing them to the fact that, later on—especially in college—they would have more opportunities to find like-minded friends.

This season proved to be a time of personal growth and character development, not to mention a lot of spiritual growth. They would say it was during this time that God truly became their "best" friend.

After a friend of mine read that story in *Boy Mom*, she told me how radical that concept was to her. "I never considered that it would be better for my kids to go through a season with no friends than to have friends who weren't great influences!" Like many parents, this compassionate mom was so concerned about her kids feeling accepted and fitting in that she'd justified the potential negative influences, hoping her son wouldn't be affected.

With this new inspiration, she started limiting her son's interactions with a specific group of boys and was surprised that, after some initial pushback from her son, she began to see a shift in his attitude and disposition. A few months later she was excited to tell me he'd even thanked her. He spent more time with the family, and he and his sister spent more time together as well—a great side benefit!

I have the advantage of seeing my two oldest boys with an incredibly full and fun social life now that they're away at college, and I can say it was worth the wait during those lonelier years. I can also say that my son who argued to hang out with the "cool kids" for a season thanked me later for making a tough parenting call in his early teenage years. He realizes that he was spared from potential trouble—or at least from some awkward situations.

He's also glad that during that season he became an excellent guitar player, surfed a lot, took up running, read a ton of books, and got more involved with the youth group, making friends with kids he hadn't been sure he would enjoy. He also survived many weekend nights hanging out with his very cool parents, even if it took him a few years to realize how cool they are!

Technology, Media, and Entertainment

We'll talk more extensively about screens in chapter 13, but let's touch on the influences of technology, media, and entertainment present now.

In 2019, the year *before* the COVID-19 pandemic hit, research by Common Sense Media showed that eight- to twelve-year-olds averaged around five hours on screens per day and teenagers seven and a half hours.[3] We know that during the pandemic, screen time across the board only increased, so it's frightening to imagine what we'll learn next. Data like this can be overwhelming, but the time our kids spend on screens is without a doubt a big shaping factor in their lives.

Screens count! As parents, we have a responsibility to know what our kids are doing online and to set firm boundaries for them. The phrase *You become like the company you keep* applies to the company kids spend time with virtually too. We need to take this seriously!

The music, shows, and other entertainment our kids choose will shape their character and their future. Be involved in these choices, Mom and Dad! You have permission to parent all of it— the earbuds and Netflix and their social media accounts. It is, in fact, your job!

I receive a lot of emails from parents upset over how much their kids choose to spend time on screens and entertainment, and I remind them what I want to remind you: *Your kids don't know how much is too much!* They don't know what's OK, normal, healthy, or excessive. They might know what their friends do, but they don't have a built-in sense of limits. That's why God gave them parents! It's our job to set limits. And though they may not show it, your kids want you to confidently tell them what is and isn't OK.

Don't shrink back from this responsibility! Step in. Talk to your kids. Offer them alternatives. Get them out of their dark dungeons (I mean, bedrooms) and into some fresh air. Sacrifice some of your own work (or, ahem, screen time) to be active with your kids. Cook together, train for a race, or visit a museum.

Unfortunately, we're quick to normalize behaviors that ought to never become normal. Yet when you zoom out and get a fresh look at your family—seeing how often everyone is isolated and staring at individual screens—it can and should be concerning. This is not what we were made for. *(I'm preaching to myself here as well. Like I said in chapter 3, I'm working on it!)*

Role Models

In a world that sometimes seems so dark and discouraging, the great news is that many bright lights are still out there—amazing role models who can impact our kids' lives in a wonderful way. Hopefully, you're part of a healthy church that has these role models as Sunday school and youth group leaders. Especially as they reach their tween and teenage years, it can be incredibly helpful for your children to have people beyond Mom and Dad speaking truth into their lives.

Side note: As with anyone you let close to your kids, do your due diligence to vet the youth leaders, coaches, and mentors your kids spend time with. While they can be the greatest gift to your child, youth work can also attract predators, and wisdom is required before allowing your kids to be alone with someone you don't know well.

We can also find incredible role models through books, movies, and story. Reading, my boys encountered heroes who died hundreds of years before they were born but felt like kindred spirits by the end of the book. Great stories inspire kids, so introduce them to plenty!

Another benefit of raising children in the world today is that we have access to inspiring people we can follow and learn from through social media or the internet. Whether your child is interested in music, sports, film, or the arts—or anything else—I guarantee you can find someone with excellent character for them to follow. Take the time to help them find quality role models.

My boys have a list of professional athletes they follow on social media who model a godly lifestyle and often offer inspiring posts. They follow musicians and pastors, skateboarders and artists, who remind them of their identity and purpose in this world. I'm so grateful for the role models my boys will probably only get to thank in heaven.

Name Your Five

Influences are shaping all of us all the time. You might have heard it said that you are the average of the five people you spend the most time with. Perhaps a helpful exercise for your family would be to consider the five people or other influences (games, YouTube channels, shows, and so on) each of you spend the most time with. Write them down. Imagine how you will look in five years if each day you become more like these five.

Maybe some of you will see a need to shift your priorities, begin looking for new friends or activities, or seek out new people to follow online. You can no doubt name some people you have great respect for, and maybe you can find a way to be in their presence—in real life or virtually—more often.

You go first, Mom and Dad. Humbly tell your kids the steps you're taking to surround yourself with positive influences, and then invite your kids to do the same!

Note: Find a Scripture-based prayer for good and godly influences in our kids' lives in the resource section.

Humbly tell your kids the steps you're taking to surround yourself with positive influences, and then invite your kids to do the same.

A Word to Dads

Your life isn't lived in a vacuum, and neither are your kids'. For better or for worse, they're being shaped by influences in the world around them. And it can be difficult for bad influences to be undone. The time you're given to spend with your kids is your biggest opportunity to manage the influences in their lives. But take note: the world is full of people with agendas, seeking to influence your kids. And in many cases, this will be in the opposite direction you know is best for them.

So be aware that there's a spiritual dimension to all this, dads. First Peter 5:8 says, "Be alert and of sober mind. Your enemy the devil prowls around like a roaring lion looking for someone to devour." Don't tune out. Keep your eyes wide open to who's in your kids' lives. Be on surveillance mode, and keep the conversation channels open. It doesn't take a lot of time, but it does take some intentionality. Ask your kids questions and then listen. Give them enough time and attention, and they'll keep talking to you, giving you a window of opportunity to speak into their lives about what and who you see influencing them.

I've had some great discussions with my kids in the realm of music and its influence. We've had open and honest discussions about vocal artists and their lyrics. In light of standards we set early on in our family, it's been awesome to watch my kids steering themselves toward music that upholds values that honor God.

We also tend to do entertainment as a family. If we stream movies, we discuss what we plan to watch and why. We've had some good family discussions about why we do or don't want to see a movie based on reviews, ratings, content, and so on. To my surprise, my kids have become great movie critics as we've made entertainment and its influence on our family a kitchen table conversation.

Beyond streaming movies and listening to music, the influences we as parents must contend with can seem overwhelming. When kids are young, we worry about them falling into a swimming pool or getting hit by a car, but as they get older, the world they live in gets more complex. So are its threats and dangers to their welfare. More than anything, the battle is about the thoughts of the mind. And this is where the influence of technology has grown exponentially in recent years.

Worrying about the influence of kids at school or in the neighborhood is now eclipsed by the internet and its social media platforms. If you're not providing your kids with the influences you desire for them in the areas of identity, sexuality, meaning, and purpose, then someone else is or soon will be. *Be the first and not the last to the table of influence in your kids' lives.* Setting limits on devices may give you a lot of help in this area.

As adults, we can easily forget that children have navigation skills still in development. Although they may look like they've mastered the tricycle in the driveway, that doesn't mean they're ready to take off down the highway on a Harley. As a parent, you're the master influencer, the coordinator of all other influences. A bit of an air traffic controller. You're guiding your kids safely through the air and steering them clear of danger.

Kids appreciate it when you care enough to protect them, though don't be surprised if they don't show it right away. The truth is, the security they find in the boundaries you lovingly set in their early years can set you up to be a trusted guide later in life.

Thoughts from Josiah, Age Twenty-Two

I had some relatively lonely years as a teenager, but the time I spent with friends was good because I spent it with the right people.

I remember spending a lot of time with my youth leader, sometimes two to three times a week. I spent some time with my peers, too, but then I phased out of some time with some of them when they started making bad decisions. Instead, I started spending more time with some of the older people who were good for me to be around because they showed me what it looked like to live a godly life a few years ahead of where I was, like going to college or having a girlfriend or a wife. It's so helpful to have a clear picture in my head of what those things should look like.

I think it would have been cool if more kids my age had been good influences for me, but that just wasn't the case. (We lived in a small community.) Yet in many ways, I'm who I am because I chose to spend time with the people I did, so I can't be disappointed about those years.

My friend Thunderstorm showed me what it was like to be a leader at youth group. He was kind and a man of integrity. Hojo helped me see what it was like to be competitive and funny as a leader. Sean showed me how to be thoughtful and curious and have opinions. He also introduced me to some of my favorite songs and movies, which was a huge blessing. Danny showed me what it was like to be a husband and a father to little kids as well as be pastoral to others. Chris was a cool godly influence in my life—a surfer, a spear fisher. Ian was a disciple maker, evangelist, a rugged dude. I always enjoyed his perspective on things.

Looking back, I see how God shaped me in unique ways with each good influence he placed in my life. And when I reflect on the intentional influences I've had in my life, I think of Psalm 1:

> Blessed is the one
>   who does not walk in step with the wicked
> or stand in the way that sinners take
>   or sit in the company of mockers,

but whose delight is in the law of the LORD,
> and who meditates on his law day and night.
That person is like a tree planted by streams of
> water,
> which yields its fruit in season
and whose leaf does not wither—
> whatever they do prospers.

Not so the wicked!
> They are like chaff
> that the wind blows away.
Therefore the wicked will not stand in the judgment,
> nor sinners in the assembly of the righteous.

For the LORD watches over the way of the righteous,
> but the way of the wicked leads to destruction.

I haven't done things perfectly, but looking back now I see how what my mom calls the "law of influence" played out in my life. I was a friend to many, but I didn't sit in the counsel of sinners. My delight was in the law of the Lord, and the fruit born in its season is the fruit I've experienced as a young adult. I am grateful.

Reflection Questions

1. Who are the closest people to your children, and do you have any concerns about their influence on them?

2. Which peer or friend influences do you see building up your children? Which ones might be dragging them down?

3. What are some steps you might take to bring helpful influences into your children's lives in the season they're in?

CHAPTER 7

HOME BASE

Make Your Home the Hub

> *If you would have your children turn out well,*
> *don't turn your home into a lunch counter and*
> *lodging house.*
>
> **—Billy Sunday**

My two oldest sons recently came home from college on a break. Before they traveled, I asked what they hoped to do while home. Josiah named a couple of people he'd like to see, but then he said, "Honestly, I just want to hang with the family. Dinners, some beach time together. That's what I miss the most."

And my life was made.

In chapter 2 we talked about the importance of parents setting a trajectory for their family—about developing a family identity and living out a purposeful destiny. Now we'll talk about what keeps kids coming home. The glue that keeps families bonded.

Not by Accident

Acts 17:26–27 says, "He marked out their appointed times in history and the boundaries of their lands. God did this so that they would seek him and perhaps reach out for him and find him, though he is not far from any one of us."

I love these verses for many reasons, but I especially love to consider how God has purposefully and creatively designed our families. Not just for us and each of our children to get through eighteen years together, but by appointment. He put us together during a specific time in history and with boundaries for us to live within. I'm awed by God's thoughtful order! It's important to know that as big or small, charming or challenging, colorful or quirky our families may be, we can trust that none of it is by chance. God is doing something on purpose here.

Families are busy. Many have kids attending different schools, sometimes in different directions. Often, Mom and Dad both work, inside or outside the home. After school, the kids have sports and clubs and jobs. Then on weekends, they want to be social—to hang out with friends. Parents have social lives and other obligations too.

When in the world will families ever truly bond if all the people in it are rarely together?

This must be worked out uniquely according to your family's circumstances, values, and priorities. But I suggest it's worth it to carve out time, purposefully and even religiously, for the family to hang out together.

If you want your family to be close, do these three things: Decide it. Expect it. Talk about it. Then do all the stuff it takes to make that closeness a reality. Over time, keep doing the stuff, both when it's easy and convenient and when it's a total pain. Making your home the hub will happen when you make it a priority.

If you want to raise kids who feel most at home *in* their home and together, then get serious about making it happen.

Here are eight ways to make your home your family's hub:

If you want to raise kids who feel most at home in their home and together, then get serious about making it happen.

1. Eat together often.

Research shows that kids who grow up with regular family dinners earn better grades, are less likely to experiment with drugs and alcohol, and have happier lives overall.[1] It's hard to imagine so many benefits from the simple act of eating meals together, but, of course, it's much more than eating a meal. It's gathering. Connecting. A safe and welcome place with food to share. Shoot for eating together anytime family members are all home.

Also avoid boring conversation and unnecessary correction or nagging at the table. Make it a pleasant experience, and kids will want more of it. Note: Find a list of conversation starters for family meals in the resource section.

2. Establish a family night.

Set aside at least one night a week for family night, then make it something your kids will look forward to. Plan a meal that's special (or at least especially delicious). If you can't cook, get takeout, or if the kids enjoy cooking, get them to help. There are no rules here. Breakfast for dinner, Costco lasagna . . . What does matter is that you're fully present. That you put your work and phone and other distractions away and commit to this being your family night.

Bonus points: An after-dinner game? An evening walk or trip out for ice cream? Gathering by a fire? We've had some epic dance parties after dinner in every season of raising kids, and while I can't say the Swansons have the gift of dance, those are some good memories.

Set the tone for lingering at the table by being prepared with some good conversation starters and lots of food. Have dessert ready to set on the table as soon as dinner is complete. (Store-bought cookies count!) Consider conversation starters or a good topic to bring up when you all sit down. You might bring up current events or something new you're learning.

3. Make your home a welcoming place.

A lot of moms and dads tell me their kids are often in their bedrooms on devices or talking to friends. The parents are frustrated that the family is fragmented. I try to follow up with those folks by asking these questions: What is the vibe when you walk into your home? Is it a comfortable, happy place? Are you around, ready to chitchat and enjoy your kids' presence? When your kids walk into the house, do they feel like they just entered a safe and happy place—a place where they're cheered on? Does it smell good and feel good? Do you play music that helps put everyone in a peaceful or upbeat mood?

Or is it dark or quiet? Do kids feel under attack the minute they enter? Is there unpleasant background noise, like the news always on the TV or something else that sets a negative tone? Are you busy staring at a computer or your phone?

I've certainly caught myself being so task oriented that I'm not creating a welcoming environment for my family. When I'm overwhelmed, I might let the house get cluttered and the fridge get bare, and there's no doubt it affects my boys' interest in hanging out. Knowing I have this tendency, I've worked on being more intentional about setting the mood in the house. I try to light some pleasant-smelling candles, turn on good music, and be there to greet my people with a hug and a listening ear. Whoa, what a difference it makes when I choose to do that.

4. Schedule in ways you can be together.

When kids are young, they're dependent on us for rides everywhere and to accompany them everywhere they go. This can be super inconvenient, I know, but later we all miss it. (Really!) In all stages, it's easy and often sensible for family members to divide and conquer. You go here, I'll go there. You grab Bobby, I'll take Sue. That's life, and sometimes it's the best way to tackle Little League and your church's midweek Awana program, ballet class and youth group.

But sometimes we can schedule our activities, appointments, and commitments in ways we can be together. Car time is a great time to talk, listen, and laugh. My husband sometimes meets the boys and me at Costco on his way home from work to "help" us shop. We don't necessarily "need" his help (shh!), but it's one more shared activity. When older kids had sports practice, I often brought the younger kids to play at the nearby playground or just watch the practice.

There's no doubt it's easier to run errands alone (and sometimes I desperately need the headspace), but it can be fun to take a couple of kids along and find a fun stop along the way. They learn character qualities like patience while Mom is at the bank or the post office. We chat or listen to a good audio book while I drive, and we get a smoothie or ice cream cone on the way home.

Again, when kids are young, togetherness seems impossible to avoid, but as they get older it's surprising how much everyone scatters. Continuing to do stuff together will require some intentionality and for sure some sacrifice, but trust me, it's worth it.

5. Make weekends mostly family time.

While weekends are a great time to do our favorite activities, a lot of families fill those days scattered at various friends' homes or doing activities *separately*. If your kids are still young, I suggest starting slow on this. The more normal it is to be together as a family, the less your kids will start to think they need to be social butterflies all the time.

Some families live in neighborhoods with playmates literally next door. That offers some serious pros and some potential cons. Let your kids know that home is their hub. Don't let them run off to play every time they want to, even though it might offer you some peace and quiet. And consider the influences they're being exposed to and make some hard choices about who they play with and where.

Meanwhile, give kids a lot of time at home, together. If you have a yard that's safe to play in, put them there and let their imaginations take over. Set them up in the house with Legos or blocks or paints or a project. My older boys will tell you their greatest childhood memories involve time playing together in our very small fenced-in yard!

6. Be one another's biggest fans!

As much as possible, expect kids to be there for each other's events. Bring them to the games, the performances, the award ceremonies. It won't always work out, and that's OK. But if you set up their absence as normal, they'll be used to it. Help them understand that a big part of being in a family is cheering for one another. They should feel good about that role. This has the potential to bring up some jealousy, but then you have a chance to walk them through that, developing more character.

You can also help your children appreciate and support *you* in what you do, Mom and Dad. I'm not sure why we tend to keep our work and interests to ourselves, but I believe it's good for kids to learn to appreciate and support their parents' interests too.

Years ago, when I was invited to run the NYC marathon

with my brother to raise funds for muscular dystrophy research, I talked about my training with my family, and they supported my efforts. When I finally got to New York to run the race, Dave and the boys gathered around the computer at home, tracking my progress and texting me encouraging messages. There's no doubt that their support helped me run—or more like limp—across the finish line!

I share book ideas and ministry plans with my boys even when I think it's not that interesting to them. Why? Because I want them to learn to listen to and care for others, and I figure their home is a good training ground. Of course, I try not to carry on too long (though that has been known to happen). I keep it as short and sweet and interesting as I can. Who knows, one day they might have a talkative spouse, and then she can thank me for teaching them to not just talk about themselves but to listen to others!

7. Establish rituals and traditions.

God created our world full of rhythms and routines. From the daily rising and setting of the sun to the seasons of the year, it seems that God placed within us a need for routines and reminders. I've witnessed this in my own children, who thrive on familiarity and routine. Even my least orderly kids have wanted to know Mom would be there to tuck them in at night and be around to hang out or make pancakes in the morning.

In his book *Habits of the Household*, Justin Whitmel Earley wrote, "One of the most significant things about any household is what is considered to be normal. Moments aggregate, and they become memories and tradition. Our routines become who we are, become the story and culture of our families."[2]

Kids may not realize the impact your daily routines will have on them until later, and that's OK. But they're likely to remind you, year after year, of the traditions you put into place for hol-idays and special occasions: "We need to get the Christmas tree the day after Thanksgiving" or "Grandma will be making apple pie for dessert, right?" At our house, birthdays begin with a box of Lucky Charms, and the new year is welcomed with a fresh jour-nal and a family worship or goal-setting night. While I've never felt like I'm great at elaborate holiday rituals, I see how even the simple ones offer my boys a sense of security.

8. Make "family" a big deal.

Remember chapter 2 and the whole thing about setting your fam-ily's trajectory? This is where it gets super practical. Talk about what makes your family your family! Be proud of your tribe. Do you gather with grandparents or FaceTime them if they're far away on Sundays? Is Friday pizza and movie night? Do you gather for football games or family devotions or chores on Saturday morn-ing? Do you love Taco Tuesday or camping out in the yard the first weekend of summer? These are all things that give your family your unique flavor. Talk about them. Celebrate them!

A Gathering Place

If your kids want to hang out with friends, you're wise to make your home a great place to do that. Do all you can to make your home the hub where your kids' friends feel welcome. Some parents think to be *that (cool) family,* you must have an awesome house and a lot of fancy toys. But that isn't true. What you do need is food, something fun to do, and most of all, a happy, welcoming environment.

If your kids want to hang out with friends, you're wise to make your home a great place to do that.

Stock up at Costco with

snack foods kids love—crackers or chips, juice, fruit, ingredients to whip up pizza. Growing kids also appreciate real meals—and often. If you have a yard, a Ping-Pong table, or a basketball hoop—even a deck of cards or some fun board games—you've got enough.

Especially when you have tweens or teens in the house, I suggest investing in fun things kids can do with friends and each other before spending money on a lot of other things. When we first moved to our home on the North Shore of Oahu, I started dreaming of a kitchen remodel right away. My husband, on the other hand, started designing a skateboarding bowl for our front yard. I can't say I was excited about the idea at first, but over time, as our kids' friends gathered at our house to skate and socialize, I realized the value of that investment. (I got my kitchen remodel ten years later.)

Our on-purpose-by-God families need our attention and care to keep being meaningful in all seasons. The great news is that it just takes simple and practical steps to get there, even if they may seem countercultural. Making your home your family's hub requires diligence, thoughtfulness, and probably a lot of pizza, but when you see your kids' smiling faces as they come home from school, happy to be in their haven, or the pride they have inviting their friends over to shoot hoops, it's worth it.

A Word to Dads

Kids will vote with their feet, so consider ways to win their votes. Part of keeping everyone together is making a place everyone wants to come to. In part, this is about making your house a home. You don't have to build an X Games Vert ramp or an award-winning tree house in your backyard, but you should pay attention to the little things that make your house a home. These are also the things that will make your grown-up kids want to come back.

Kids need fun things to do with you and the rest of the family. And you don't even need much space. As I write, from a small room next to me I hear my kids battling in a chess tournament. The board and seating takes up less than three feet of square space. All it took was some intentional time on a Walmart trip to buy the chess set and add it to the small stack of board games we've collected over time.

Earlier tonight, we were having a family dinner with all members in attendance, including Grandma and Grandpa. Of course, a family dinner involves preparation and clean up, and everyone can help. Eating a meal together around a table is key to making your home the hub. It took a little coordination and planning and yelling "Come and eat!" about ten times, but it happened, and the conversations were great. We covered highlights of the day, and we reminisced about family vacations.

Just before dinner, as I cheered him on, our youngest, Levi, spent several minutes in a jumping challenge to see if he could touch a beam that spans across the ceiling of our living room. I stopped some work I was doing to take a little interest in his endeavor, then ran and got a tape measure to determine just how high his new record-setting feat was. We talked about the nuances of jumping. Better to jump off one foot or both? Running start or not?

Looking back on the evening, I can see how, with a little intentionality, the "hub" of home can be a stage for even the spontaneous unfolding of family life and interactions so crucial to our kids' lives. This wasn't a monumental night, a holiday, or anything that will go into our photo album, but I'm pretty sure this is the stuff that will be part of my kids' idea of what home means to them.

Thoughts from Luke, Age Eighteen

I'm a competitive surfer, but I love watching team sports. One thing I notice is that in the middle of any type of game, teams must regroup in some sort of huddle or team meeting. They can't stay on the field (or the court and so on) forever or they'd get tired and confused and lose track of their game plan.

When a team comes together, a lot of little things happen essential to making it through the game. Players down some water, wipe off their sweat, slap each other on the back, and listen to the coach reminding them of the game plan. Those who've been on the bench are part of the huddle too. They're part of the team.

Our family huddles up in our own way, regularly. Coming back together is important so we can remind one another what we're doing, how much we care about one another, and what our goals are. We're refreshed and grounded when we connect at home.

We all get busy, and we've all been going different directions. I travel a lot for surfing, and sometimes I'm gone for many weeks at a time. But when we get back together and sit down for a meal or a family night, I feel the difference. This is what family is to me. It's my grounding. It feels safe and comfortable, and I'd even say it feels necessary for me to go out and do the other things I do.

Reflection Questions

1. How often does your family gather around the table together? Is this or something else an area in which you might improve?

2. How does your living situation (neighborhood and so on) affect your family life? Where might you make adjustments so you regroup together at home more often?

3. Which rituals, traditions, and routines define your family the most? What are some you'd like to add to your family's rhythm?

CHAPTER 8

NOS AND YESES

Parent with Your Kids' Very Best in Mind

*If any of you lacks wisdom, you should ask God,
who gives generously to all without finding fault,
and it will be given to you.*

—James 1:5

Consider the original garden, Eden, where God was the original parent and Adam and Eve were the first children. God gave a lot of big yeses right from the start there. And he gave one hard no. In fact, he put that no smack in the center of the garden.

Some serious parenting was going on there, and I don't want anyone to miss it.

God does all things with intention and nothing by chance. He set things up with purpose. Like me, at some point you might have asked why God would create the Tree of Knowledge of Good and Evil, put a big no on it, and then place it right in the middle of the garden. Or why he put his first children in such a perfect place, then put a no in the center with so much potential for things to go wrong.

To understand that, it helps to ask what parents want most for themselves and for their children. I think we would agree they want their children to know how much they love them, for their children to love them back, and for their children to trust them.

No one needs to teach us that; it's in our DNA. As the original parent, God wanted the same things. He showed his children his love by giving them life and providing them with wonderful things—his presence to boot. In his wisdom, he then created a situation with many yeses *and the one hard no*. He was giving his children an opportunity to experience his love and to love and trust him in return.

As parents, we get to say yes to our kids, often. Saying yes to a hug or a treat or an opportunity or an adventure may be one of the sweetest parts of parenting. Yet we also give our kids some hard nos. Some that they understand and some they don't understand, at least yet.

They may understand why they shouldn't touch a hot stove, but they may not understand why they can't just turn on a burner if they promise not to touch it. As a parent, you have reasons for saying no; you understand things your children don't. Something might be near the stove that could catch fire, or you think your child might forget and leave the burner on.

There are plenty of dangers kids simply do not understand yet. But what the parent wants is for their children to be so confident in their love for them that they will obey them out of trust. These parent-child interactions are profound opportunities to prepare our children for a life of faith.

Parental Wiring

We all have our natural bent as parents. God designed us that way. So let me first say that if you're a natural at saying no and setting boundaries, well done. I imagine you're a mature, wise parent who's well equipped to raise amazing kids. We might need to nudge you to look for opportunities to say yes a little more so your nos really count, but we'll get to that a little later.

Meanwhile, I confess that I'm a yes-loving parent by nature. I love to make my kids happy, and I enjoy giving them what they love the most. I'm pretty comfortable with a bit of junk food. I'm not too strict about screen time or bedtimes. I mean, I set rules where they're needed (see previous chapters), but when our kids are making good choices overall, I love to bless them with things I remember loving as a child. *Donuts included.*

Dave, on the other hand, is generally less worried about making the kids happy in the present. Also, he's a doctor. So while I'm quick to give a yes on occasional soda or a sugary treat, Dave is 100 percent comfortable with a swift no. And this goes way beyond junk food. When we face difficult parenting decisions about entertainment or money management, and I'm all caught up in my boys' *happiness level*, I'm ultimately grateful for Dave's wise, objective leadership.

What I'm saying here is if you happen to be a fellow yes-loving parent, *I get you*. I prefer giving a cheerful yes to a no, any day. And you'll appreciate the last part of this chapter. But I've become convinced that learning the heart and art of saying no is the difference between paradise and exile. We'll have lots of great opportunities to give our kids healthy yeses, but we're also wise to learn from my husband—as well as from science and the Bible—that saying no to our kids is foundational to their faith and essential for building truly amazing character.

What's So Good about Saying No?

If we earthly parents can teach our kids that our saying no is one of the most important parts of our love/trust relationship with them, we're setting them up to know and understand their relationship with their heavenly Father. I want my kids to experience the blessing of living under the authority of someone who has more wisdom and understanding than they do. And, ultimately, I want all of this to prepare them to grow into a relationship with their heavenly Father where no is respected, heeded, and even—as hard as it might be in the moment—*appreciated*.

I'm convinced that one of the most holy jobs we have as parents is to be a representation of God until our kids are old enough to understand and relate directly to their Father in heaven. (We'll never do this perfectly, but we can hope!) A child who doesn't hear no enough or isn't required to submit to a no at home is being set up for a shaky walk with their heavenly Father when they're released from the authority of their parents. I shudder at the thought even as I struggle to practice this concept in my home.

A child who doesn't hear no enough or isn't required to submit to a no at home is being set up for a shaky walk with their heavenly Father.

While my highest motivation for offering firm nos is to train my child's heart to obey and trust God, plenty more reasons why hearing no is good for our kids exist. In an article in *Psychology Today*, Dan Mager wrote, "Believe it or not, parents do their children a tremendous disservice when they don't give them the experience of being told 'no' . . . Learning how to deal with not getting what you want and when you want it is an essential skill that everyone needs to develop."[1]

Especially for us yes-loving parents, the following four practical reasons kids need plenty of nos might be helpful:

1. Saying no is crucial for kids' safety and well-being.

Parents, your kids have no idea how dangerous the world is, and
if they're left to their own reasoning, they're likely to end up in
some dire straits. When they're young, kids face danger in the way
of simple things like hot stoves and busy streets and strangers.
Even an otherwise logical teenager might make poor decisions
under stress, because the prefrontal cortex, the part of the brain
responsible for using good judgment, doesn't fully develop until
the mid-twenties.[2] (As I write this, my twenty-two-year-old just
broke his arm jumping into a skate bowl—on a mattress. Thanks
for helping make my point, son.)

2. Saying no helps kids feel secure.

Kids of all ages feel most secure when we let them know what's OK
and what's not. Children don't inherently know these things, but
what a relief they experience when their parents do. Boundaries
are a blessing.

I've heard the example of observing the behavior of children in a playground. When there's a fence around it, they will
play all the way up to the fence line, using every bit of space
available to them. Yet if there's no fence, they stay close to their
home base, unlikely to venture far. This is a good picture of
what boundaries do for children. Boundaries give them a "safe
space" to explore.

In *Boy Mom*, I refer to what I call the "unexpected power of
'no.'" When they're young, kids depend on Mom and Dad to guide
them in both little and big choices. As they hit their teenage years,
they continue to look to their parents to help them navigate. Even
when they act like they know what they're doing, much of the

time they're just figuring it out as they go. Our kids may ask permission to do many things, but in reality, they may not feel ready to do those very things. I've learned that a no from Mom and Dad is often a relief, even to a teenager.

3. Saying no teaches kids the value of delayed gratification.

Accepting the value of delayed gratification is one of the most important character qualities our kids can develop, and it's sadly lacking in many young people today. When I consider my husband's success in many areas of life—from his education and job to his hard work and faithfulness to our family—I recognize that his willingness to delay gratification has been a huge key to all of it. Without a doubt, this began with some firm nos in his childhood.

In his book *Your Future Self Will Thank You*, author Drew Dyck wrote, "Self-control isn't just one good character trait, a nice addition to the pantheon of virtues. It's foundational. Not because it's more important than other virtues, but because the others rely upon it."[3]

Our modern world has conditioned kids to expect things to come to them easily and instantly. For our children to learn patience, resilience, and the value of delayed gratification, we must look for ways to help them learn to wait for—and to even go without—something they want.

Our kids need to understand that what they want *most* may require giving up what they want *now*. And this concept is best learned through a lot of practice.

I'm further motivated in this area by the self-control theory of crime, which suggests that how kids are parented up until the age of ten impacts their level of self-control. And low levels of self-control are correlated with criminal and impulsive conduct.[4]

4. Saying no prepares kids for the real world.

When we give our children what they want too often, we may think we're making their life easy. But instead we're setting them up for some harsh realities ahead. When we offer them nos at the right times and for the right reasons, we're helping them learn to live without things their "flesh" so desires. This prepares them for the very real temptations and challenges in the real world they must live in.

Robin Berman, author of *Permission to Parent*, said, "If children don't hear 'no' at home, imagine how it will feel when they hear it in the workplace. . . . Protective parenting has created children who feel entitled and who are psychologically fragile because they have too much power and lack resilience because they've never experienced failure."[5]

As convinced as you may be that saying no is good for kids, if you still struggle to follow through, you're not alone.

Why It's Hard to Say No

Here are some of the reasons we don't want to say no to our kids.

- We want them to be our friends and fear that saying no might make them dislike us. (This one hits close to home for me!) In his book *Revolutionary Parenting*, George Barna suggests we ought to gamble on the long-term goals over the short-term, feel-good outcome: "I have come to realize that rather than being accepted as an adult 'best friend' of my children, my most important role is to be a trusted adviser and confidant."[6] I like that perspective.
- Not wanting to say no to our kids is a simple desire to avoid the fallout. (The drama can be very real.) Hang in there, grown-ups. We can do hard things.

- Sometimes we feel sorry for our kids—for any variety of reasons. They may be lonely, they may struggle with school or relationships, or (fill in the blank). For all these reasons, they need our empathy. Yet don't for a minute think that saying yes to things you don't feel good about will help them. Keep your head, Mom and Dad.

- We often feel guilty about our circumstances and want to find ways to compensate for our lack of involvement in our kid's life or some other area of neglect. It's important to acknowledge these feelings, but don't let them steer you.

- Finally, we may want our kids to have a better childhood than we had. There's nothing wrong with that, but be wise with this impulse. You can give them a better childhood in many ways without indulging them in areas you know in your right mind aren't helpful. Stay strong, folks.

The Art of Saying No to Kids

Since saying no is part of our job as parents, we're wise to handle the task with care. A few ideas can certainly make our "no job" a bit more palatable for all parties.

First, no is best received within a healthy relationship with our kids. When they know we love and enjoy them, when we have healthy communication and mutual respect, our nos will be received in a totally different light than if we don't have a good relationship. Always make the effort to build that relationship with your child in all seasons.

Next, a learned skill in parenting is worthy of some practice. It's an objective approach I simply call the Three Cs: calm, calculated, confident. First, we must be calm, refusing to get caught up in our emotions or theirs. Then considering the circumstances in the time available to us, we must calculate the best response. It may not be perfect, but it ought to be thoughtful and wise. Finally, we move forward confidently. Lovingly tell your child "No," "Not yet," or perhaps "I need time to think about this." As my friend in the military says, "We do not negotiate with terrorists" (which sometimes come in the form of toddlers and teenagers).

By now you've probably learned that if you start hedging on a response, kids will eat you alive. At some point my husband and I realized our youngest son was getting good at bulldozing his way through our no decisions and finding a way to turn them into an exhausted, "OK, whatever." We weren't proud of that discovery (the kid's got skills!), and we had some backpedaling to do. We sat down with him and re-articulated our God-given authority and the expectation of respect and obedience on his part. And let's be real here: we're still a work in progress!

Parents, we must stay in authority. This doesn't mean you'll always get it right, and it's OK if you don't. But the Three Cs will help you parent from an emotionally responsible place.

While sometimes a firm no without explanation is reasonable, most often our children want and deserve at least a brief explanation for it. Kids will also be more cooperative when they understand the why behind the no. But try to avoid lecturing or long explanations that only invite an argument. Instead, make it clear that you have a good reason and aren't just trying to ruin all their fun.

Be careful of those gifted negotiators. There's a slippery slope when we start to give in. But if you're firm and hold to the limits you set consistently, your kids will progressively learn to accept those limits and submit to your authority.

On the other hand, if you say no initially but then relent because your kids wear you down, in essence you've taught them if they just cry, beg, or plead *long enough*, eventually you'll give in. I've learned this the hard way.

Reverse Negotiation

Since my youngest is such a gifted negotiator, I've been putting "reverse negotiation" into practice. I learned this process from Robin Berman, the author of *Permission to Parent*.[7] Reverse negotiation is responding to a child's refusal to submit by going in the opposite direction. If our children ask for something and we say no, but they ask again (or use any tactic to keep pushing), we give them the opposite of their request.

For example, Levi asks for a piece of candy. I say, "No, but you can have one for dessert after dinner."

He says, "But, Mom, I ate a really good lunch, and I did my chores, and—"

I stop him and say, "Now you won't get dessert after dinner. Sorry, buddy, but my no means no."

This "ought to" put an end to things and teach a mildly painful lesson. But if he happens to be crazy enough to keep arguing, my job is to keep moving in the reverse direction, with something like, "OK, now no sweets tomorrow as well," which would be a very sad two days for our sugar-loving child.

Reverse negotiation is magical. You must be all-in if you use it—and I hope you will.

When, Then, and Alternatives

One of the most effective ways I've found to be objective in my parenting is offering a "when, then" response to my kids' requests. This is useful if there's a yes available *eventually*, but something else must come first, even if the yes is in the distant future.

For example, if a child wants to go outside to play with a neighbor, you might say, "Yes, when you finish your homework and chores, then you can go play." The point is to put the responsibility on their shoulders to earn privileges, not simply expect them. This is a great life principle to grow up with.

Using "when, then" can also simplify kids' incessant pleas for screen time or anything else. In *Habits of the Household*, Justin Whitmel Earley explains how he and his wife simplify parenting by having regular routines in place each week. For example, Friday night is movie night. When the kids ask him or his wife if they can watch a movie on Tuesday, their simple reply is, "Is it Friday?" *Genius!*[8]

It can be helpful to have some alternatives to offer our kids. Perhaps you say no to a sleepover at a friend's house, but you're willing to pick them up at 10:00 or 11:00 p.m. so they can have a fun evening anyway. Or maybe a no right now is more of a "Not now." You might suggest that if your daughter is still passionate about her new dance class in two months, you'll invest in new dance shoes for her. You can use your kids' wants as a reward for desired behavior or hard work.

Setting limits in parenting can be difficult, and sometimes kids do not respect or obey the boundaries we set. This is where consequences and discipline come into play. To offer some encouragement and expert guidelines on discipline, I wrote a bonus chapter, "Motivating Change: A Guide for Using Consequences and Discipline in Parenting." Find a link to it in the resource section.

If two parents are involved, obviously it's important for them to agree when it comes to setting and enforcing limits. Conflict between parents will often cause them to undermine each other and sends mixed and confusing messages to their kids. Kids also quickly learn how to play one parent against the other and manipulate when parents aren't on the same team. Regardless of your differences, it's in the best interest of your kids to try to be on the same team when it comes to yeses and nos.

Yes!

Finally, to the fun part. Yes is good too! Second Corinthians 1:20 says, "No matter how many promises God has made, they are 'Yes' in Christ. And so through him the 'Amen' is spoken by us to the glory of God."

God is also a God of yeses, and we should be parents who are generous with our yeses too! God isn't a killjoy or sitting up in heaven looking for ways to ruin our fun. Instead, he's crazy about us, and he wants to bless his children with good things. I love when the psalmist says, "You provide a broad path for my feet" (Ps. 18:36). This reminds me of how many options and opportunities we have to live freely while being in God's will. A life of faith ought never be dull.

I love to consider all the things kids can do without many limits—or in many cases, without much supervision! In our family we say yes to a lot of outdoor adventures, music and art, reading, building, and use of the imagination!

I'm a big believer in giving kids enough good, healthy freedoms that they don't have a lot of time to wish they could be staring at a screen or getting into trouble. Though some of this will depend on where you live—the climate, safety, and what kind of opportunities are available—all families should be able to find some way to allow their kids to spread their wings and have a healthy adventure. Note: In the resources section, you'll find a link to a list called "100 Things Kids Can Do Indoors without a Screen."

I encourage you to say yes to adventures and healthy activities. Say yes to wanna-be chefs making messes and to all the art projects. Say yes to obstacle courses and blanket forts and sleeping under the stars whenever possible. Say yes to trying a new sport, a new job, or serving in some way that might stretch your comfort zone but will no doubt inspire growth in your child.

In their early teenage years, both of my first two sons spent a month in Indonesia with a local surf ministry. The group is for college students and young adults but welcomes younger adventurers. Though my momma heart was still nervous, we did our due diligence to check out the leadership team and felt confident that our boys were ready. On the trip, they served poor communities, did physical labor, slept on the deck of a boat, went spear fishing, and surfed waves in the middle of the Indian Ocean. They came back more confident and spiritually mature than when they left. They were also grateful for a warm shower and Mom's cooking!

With the Lord as our best role model for parenting, we should be thoughtful about all our yeses and nos. If you get stuck trying to decide whether to give a yes or a no, ask God. He promises to give you wisdom when you ask (James 1:5)! We won't always get it right, but his grace is abundant, and he'll continue to steer us as we seek his ways.

We should always check our motives. Are we hungry for power? Or taking outside frustrations out on our kids by trying to control them? Are we being lazy and saying yes to things we truly don't think are best for our kids? Choosing our yeses and nos carefully and following through diligently will pay off in dividends with amazing kids and a more peaceful home.

Choosing our yeses and nos carefully and following through diligently will pay off in dividends with amazing kids and a more peaceful home.

A Word to Dads

Dads, we have a big assignment: being the traffic light for our kids. They need to know when something is OK and when it's not. Early in their lives, a no is used largely for safety and behavior modification. ("No, don't run in the street!" or "No, don't bite your sister!") Your instinct as a parent is to provide and protect. You're looking out for their best interests. In some cases, you're just trying to keep them from serious injury or death!

But as you do, you're teaching your kids to obey you and understand the principles of boundary and the lines between good and bad, right and wrong. This will shape them as they grow as well as their trajectory as they navigate the stop signs of life.

The Bible backs this reality of life being tied to obeying parents: "'Honor your father and mother'—which is the first commandment with a promise—'so that it may go well with you and that you may enjoy long life on the earth'" (Eph. 6:2–3). Obedience is about honor. This command is directed at children, but parents are the object of the statement. You are the key to the equation. Have these conversations with your kids! That's part of your job.

We need to give our children a lot of yeses as well as nos. Whether your kids are thrill-seekers or more cautious, some part of them will always be considering if Dad would feel good about what they're doing. Your vote of confidence—"You've got this! I believe in you!"—may be one of the most powerful things your kids will ever hear.

Getting kids to tune in to yes and no protects not only their physical body but their hearts and minds. As parents, our heart's desire is to see our kids succeed. We really want them to do well in their jobs, in their marriages, and in building their own families one day. Helping your children set their lives on a foundation of desire to make right choices is where it all begins. God's promise to us as parents is that this will, indeed, set them up for success.

> My son, do not forget my teaching,
>   but keep my commands in your heart,
> for they will prolong your life many years
>   and bring you peace and prosperity. (Prov. 3:1–2)

Thoughts from Levi, Age Twelve

The topic of this chapter is probably the hardest for me, but my mom said I should say a few things about it anyway. The truth is obedience is hard. I like it when my parents say yes, because I like to get my own way. Sometimes they say no, but I keep asking, hoping to wear them out. I'm working on obeying better.

My parents tell me often that blessings come from obeying. I know it makes God happy and it makes my parents happy, but sometimes it's hard for me to see that it makes me happier. But if I'm honest, I believe it does, mostly because I've seen that happen with my brothers, all older than me.

I know my parents told my brothers yes or no carefully, and now my brothers tell me they're blessed because of it. They all have good opportunities and a good life, and my parents tell me a lot of that is because they've honored their parents and God.

My brothers also all have a good friendship with my parents, and I think that's because they grew up trusting them when they said yes or no. Now my parents don't tell them what to do very much because they get to make their own choices. I look forward to that, but in the meantime, I know I have more work to do.

Reflection Questions

1. As a parent, does it come easier to you to say yes or to say no? Think about why that is (how you were raised, your personality, and so on).

2. In which area of parenting do you think some healthy nos would benefit your child?

3. In which area of parenting do you think some healthy yeses would benefit your child?

CHAPTER 9

DISH DUTY

Make Character a Really Big Deal

Good, honest, hardheaded character is a function of the home. If the proper seed is sown there and properly nourished for a few years, it will not be easy for that plant to be uprooted.
—**George A. Dorsey**

It's been a few years, but I well remember that New Year's Day plan to meet at the beach for the moms to chat and their kids to play. I was the last to join the small pack of women under umbrellas with towels and beach bags scattered in the sand. My older three sons, ages fifteen, thirteen, and eleven, took off for the water, where their friends had already gathered. My youngest, Levi, plopped down next to me with his favorite green toy tractor in his hand.

I exchanged "Happy New Year" greetings with everyone, though my not-so-happy mood must have been obvious since one of the women asked, "Rough morning?"

I nodded and sighed.

"Those preschool years are exhausting," one of them offered empathetically.

I laughed. "Actually, it's not my youngest—not that *he's easy*—but I'm really frustrated with that second son of mine," nodding toward Jonah. "By the time we left home this morning, he'd already complained about breakfast, started a fight with his brother, and made Levi cry. I'm determined to work on his character, but, man, I'm frustrated."

One of the moms tried to cheer me with, "Well, he's a teenager now! You might just get used to it!"

Everyone shifted their gaze to the ocean or their phones, and I got the hint that I was killing the Happy New Year vibes. Yet I didn't want to leave the conversation on that note. Even if it was just for me, I added one last comment—more like a declaration: "Well, I don't want to accept that the teenage years have to be like this. I don't want to get used to it. I want to raise kids to have great character, and I believe they can."

While the other moms awkwardly looked away, one of them, a younger mom with three small children, looked me straight in the eyes and, with a gentle smile, nodded slowly as she mouthed two little words: "Me too."

She had no idea how much I needed that support and affirmation. How good it felt to think I wasn't the only mom on the planet still holding on to hope that we might raise kids with decent character, even in the world today.

I had my work cut out for me, that's for sure. And there were no guarantees that my efforts would pay off. But I would keep hoping. And in that moment, it felt good to know I wasn't alone.

The very next day I began to implement something I called "Character Training" with that son, a daily exercise that over time helped shape his character and I honestly believe changed the course of his life. That training was so helpful that it inspired a chapter in *Boy Mom* and later my online Character Training Course, which has now helped parents all over the world in the character development of their children.

I'll be sharing more about that later in this chapter, but now I want to be clear that, next to faith, nothing I can recommend you focus on is more important than your children's character. Whatever age they are, you still have the opportunity to teach and train your kids in character. And I hope this chapter helps!

I confess, when my kids were younger, I mostly wanted them to behave well for my own comfort and convenience. I wanted them to make me look good in front of others. As they grew up, I wanted my sons to be respectful and follow instructions. And honestly, I wanted them to do the dishes without being asked! I figured that if my kids would just do what I wanted them to, we could all have a more peaceful life.

While there's some truth to that (am I right?), time taught me that character is much more than behavior modification. I learned to shift my focus from my kids' external actions to their hearts.

As my boys grew up, I realized they would ultimately have to choose the kind of character they wanted to embrace for themselves. I had to let go of control and let consequences do more of the teaching. My role was shifting from Mommy to mentor and coach.

I'm beyond happy to say that my three oldest boys are now young men who demonstrate really great character. Seriously, I only wish you could meet them! Of course, they're not perfect (only their mom is, *wink*), but they are great young men following God and making good, hard choices that make me so proud.

And yet I have a twelve-year-old who's keeping me on my toes. And might I add, humble. I'll share more on that in a bit as well, but let's just say my work is far from done.

In this chapter we'll talk about the practical things I've done and I'm still doing to train my kids to grow in character. But most importantly, we'll talk about how to motivate our children to choose to embrace the kind of character that will lead to future success and a fulfilling life.

Start Them Young

The best time to start focusing on character development is as soon as possible. Little kids are quick to learn manners. We teach them to say "Please" and "Thank you," to share, and to help take care of their toys. This all sounds easy enough, but you've probably already learned that kids aren't born with an inclination toward good manners. In fact, quite the opposite is true. None of us have had to teach a toddler to say "Mine!" or "No!" Selfishness and obstinance are part and parcel of our (sin) nature.

The best time to start focusing on character development is as soon as possible.

It's our job as parents to instruct our kids in right behaviors and to train them how to act—over and over (and over and over, ad nauseum).

More important than what we teach our kids is what we show them. This theme of modeling is important enough to reiterate it in every chapter of this book, but on the topic of character it's essential. We can teach our kids about character until we're blue in the face, but if we're not living out the character qualities we teach them, our efforts will be in vain. Kids are much more likely to grow up to do what we do than simply what we say. (Revisit chapter 3 for more on this!)

Kids Don't Know Until We Tell Them

Kids are also not born with an understanding of what character is and why it matters. They don't know *until they're taught*. So we ought to begin talking to our kids about character qualities from a young age.

A small but powerful shift I've found is using "character words" throughout the day. This is done simply by teaching your children a character quality, then looking for opportunities to incorporate those words throughout the day. You might bring up a word like *kindness* to your toddler or elementary-age child. Then look for an example of kindness in a story or in your daily life. Catch your child acting kindly and compliment them on it. Then when the time comes to correct children for an unkind act, they should have a good idea where they went wrong.

You might highlight a character quality each week or go over a list of character traits and focus on one or two at a time. Then use those words in place of more vague or general directions or corrections.

Remember how Proverbs 22:6 says, "Train up a child in the way he should go" (ESV)? Training is *teaching and practicing right behavior* rather than simply *reacting to wrong behavior*.

Here are more examples:

Bring up the word patient. Talk about what it means. Read or tell a story about someone who had to be patient. Many books highlight patience! Joseph in the book of Genesis lived a life that required much patience. (God is patient with us!) You might bake cookies and talk about how we must "wait patiently" for good things to cook. Then later in the day, when your child impatiently grabs a toy from their sibling, instead of reacting with, "Quit grabbing from your brother!" you might say, "Let's try that again! Show me what it looks like to wait *patiently* for that toy." Then still later you might "catch" your son or daughter being patient as they wait for a snack, and you can name it—tell them how much you appreciate seeing that character quality!

Bring up the word brave. Talk to your child about what it means to be *brave*. Read about Daniel in the lions' den or about Queen Esther going before King Xerxes in the Bible. If something typically makes your child fearful, you might role play how to be brave in that situation. Then look for opportunities to notice and affirm how "brave" your child is the next time you see even a seed of bravery.

Bring up the words hard work. Look for a character in a story, movie, or the Bible who is hardworking. Offer your child a chance to do a chore and then show them what hard work would look like. (Dramatize the difference between lazily wiping a counter and scrubbing it with enthusiasm—and joy!) Then catch them working hard at something—learning to ride a bike, doing a puzzle, or making their bed—and call it hard work.

The common denominator here is that rather than parenting in reaction to problems or bad behavior, you're being proactive and purposeful. And I've discovered a bonus: being purposeful makes parenting a lot more fun.

Resources Are Your Friends

Books, movies, games, and other resources are incredibly helpful in teaching character. (See the list of books and Bible stories in the resources section at the back of this book to help you get started.)

Reading books to your children and then discussing both the bad and good character qualities you see in them will make the ideas you've taught "stick" and help them transfer those qualities into their actual life. The Bible is full of stories that highlight godly character—or lack of it. Use examples from stories, movies, and real-life encounters to springboard into age-appropriate conversations about what you observe.

Their Job and Your Job

Young kids are often quite willing to at least give manners a try. They'll sing the clean-up song while picking up their toys and perform for the praise of their parents and grandparents. Eventually, though, they grow up and discover their free will—and with it the thrill of independence. This is when we can see bratty attitudes, meanness, or full-on tantrums (in public when convenient). Let's face it—the joy of using good manners dulls in comparison to the rush of Cheerios dumping or door slamming.

While none of us enjoy going head-to-head with a toddler, it's helpful to think of these encounters as "teachable moments." The key is to determine not to be caught off guard. Despite the halo design on the cover of this book, none of us are raising angels. We're raising small humans with a sin nature, so prepare yourself accordingly! Expect the resistance. Anticipate the tantrums. Like my friend Wendy Speake said on one of my podcasts, "It's your five-year-old's job to act like a five-year-old . . . and it's your job to parent them through it!"

Work, Works

Character is best built through doing hard things. Simple chores can begin young, and by the time they're teenagers kids should be well on their way to mastering the skills and tasks required for adulthood. We'll dive much deeper into this topic in the next chapter, but I can't say enough about the importance of giving kids work to do.

I also recommend training kids to do their chores routinely, without constant reminders. Kids who help around the house regularly begin to take pride in a job well done, and from my experience, being involved in housekeeping causes them to be aware and concerned about the tidiness of the whole house. It's a great feeling to see a kid humming a happy tune while doing their chores with excellence. It may take some time and consistency to get to this point, but it is worth the work and the wait. And while dishes may not be the end-all to good character, I hope you'll join me in celebrating that satisfying moment of catching your kids(s) doing the dishes, without being asked. Note: I hope you'll use the hashtag #raisingamazing to share some of your kids' shining moments on social media. More about that in the resource section at the end of the book.

As our kids hit their teenage years, we told them it was time to start looking for a job outside of the house. Our oldest two boys were initiated into the service world by washing dishes at a local restaurant. It was intensely hard work, but, boy, did it make them grow. The restaurant owners were no-nonsense men who ran a tough ship, and Josiah and Jonah quickly had the chance to put into practice character qualities we taught them at home: being on time, working hard, submitting to authority, and always going the extra mile. The jobs helped them grow in many ways, with humility at the top of the list.

Motivation for Character Development

Perhaps your kids don't like doing dishes—or like their siblings. Perhaps they're not motivated to get a job done or to do much of anything, and all my peppy talk about character only makes you discouraged. If so, you're not alone; this is not uncommon. But I also want to help you help your kids, so let's move on to the heart behind a life of character.

While we can teach manners and good behavior to our young children, and we can require work of our tweens and teens, ultimately, they'll have to decide whether they want to embrace good character for themselves. This means a great part of our job, especially as kids grow older, is to motivate them to want to have great character. To connect the dots between what they do and who they are now, and how it will impact their future.

I believe this begins with some honest, loving conversations with our kids. We need to tell them, plainly, that good, strong character will be the key to most of what they want in life. Good character is necessary to do well in school, because getting good grades requires hard work and self-discipline, and choosing not to take shortcuts or cheat is a matter of integrity.

Strong character helps build better relationships and marriages. While it's not too difficult to be kind to someone you see for only a few minutes a day, close friendship and family relationships will prove if you have the qualities of patience, kindness, and long-suffering, to name just a few.

Character is the key to success in sports. Practice requires hard work and discipline. Teamwork requires humility and cooperation. Competition shows whether you can win—and lose—well and treat even your adversary with respect.

Employers are looking to hire people with strength of character. Warren Buffett said, "In looking for people to hire, you look for three qualities: integrity, intelligence, and energy. And if they don't have the first, the other two will kill you."[1] Strong leaders and successful businesses recognize that it's easier to train a person of good character than to develop character in a skilled but unprincipled employee.

In my online Character Training Course, I emphasize that good character matters in life because the choices our kids make today will impact their future. Wise decisions have rewards, but poor decisions have consequences that can spoil future opportunities.

Recently I told my youngest son he needs to work on his character even for the simple reason of establishing good friendships. "People don't like brats, so don't be one." (Too blunt?) Having good character is good and right, but it's also practical: good character really does make your life better!

Embracing true character is challenging, though. Our kids' character will be tested every day. Compromise will seem justifiable. They'll be presented with every excuse to cheat or lie or give up and walk away, and the culture will often cheer them on as they do.

If you've ever tried to "be good" by sheer grit and determination, you may have experienced what I have: it's not sustainable. But the good news is that as Christ followers, we have an opportunity to embrace character that goes way beyond behavior. A heart transformed by the love of God not only has a deeper conviction for embracing character but also has the Holy Spirit to do the work in us. Our kids don't simply need behavior modification; they need godly character informed by God and lived out through his Spirit.

In Matthew 12:35, Jesus says, "A good man brings good things out of the good stored up in him, and an evil man brings evil things out of the evil stored up in him." My greatest goal in this chapter and in all I do is to help our kids fulfill their highest calling—having character that comes from a heart that loves God and aims to please him.

Galatians 5:22–23 lists the "fruit" of the Spirit: "love, joy, peace, forbearance, kindness, goodness, faithfulness, gentleness and self-control." The thing with fruit is that it grows naturally from the inside out. You won't get an apple from a peach tree, and grapes can't grow without a healthy vine. In the same way, true character—like love, joy, peace, and so on—grows naturally from a heart that's been transformed by God's Spirit.

In Matthew 7:16, Jesus says, "By their fruit you will recognize them," referring to false prophets. But godly character looks like fruit too! It isn't forced or contrived. It grows from the heart. The kind of character I hope we all aim for in our kids is the kind that grows naturally out of a sincere relationship with God.

Does this mean if our kids know and love God, they won't have to work at character development? I only wish! No, just like you and me, kids will still need to discipline themselves, form habits, and surrender their will daily. But the motivation is different. And the power to do the work is a game changer.

Josiah has told me that, during high school, his greatest motivation for embracing character was not Mom and Dad or consequences and discipline but his belief that God was with him.

The best way to inspire character in our kids is to inspire faith in our kids.

So as you apply everything we're discussing, please mentally add the word *heart* before every mention of the word *character*. There's nothing wrong with teaching good behavior, and a child who knows how to act will have many advantages in life. But the greatest goal in our parenting should be to raise kids with character that flows from a heart that wants to honor God. So if your child hasn't yet begun a personal relationship with Jesus, I encourage you to make that your greatest priority and prayer.

> *The greatest goal in our parenting should be to raise kids with character that flows from a heart that wants to honor God.*

Unique Circumstances, Unique Children

Many of you have heard my older sons on my podcast or have now heard stories about them through my writing or social media. I'm super grateful that my two boys in college love God and have chosen to pursue a character-rich life. My third son is now navigating his way through the world of professional surfing, staying true to his faith and godly character in what can be a very dark culture. That's three down, one to go.

You also know I have a younger son who at age twelve is still growing up. He brings me so much joy and laughter, but there's no doubt that his character is a work in progress. We're focusing a lot these days on respect, emotional regulation, thoughtfulness, and patience, just to name a few.

We must consider many factors that shape our children. For instance, Levi's early years looked very different from his brothers' in a number of ways:

Birth order. The youngest children in the family are often known for being more spoiled, entitled, and attention-seeking than their older siblings. Not an excuse, but a tendency for us to be aware of.

Technology. Whereas my older boys were raised with very little technology until their late elementary years or tweens, Levi has never known a world without smartphones. Technology is a factor for most of our kids' character development today.

Parenting. (Gulp.) I began blogging the year Levi was born. By the time he was a toddler, I was putting many hours into my online work. There's no doubt that I was more distracted while parenting him than I was when his older brothers were young. I'm owning this now.

Birth order. I know, I already said this one, but a child's birth order affects him or her in so many ways. To Levi's advantage, though, he has incredible older sibling role models who set great examples for his character and faith. (They've also done a lot for him when Mom and Dad were busy.)

When Levi was still quite young, I was struggling with the reality of how different his upbringing was from his brothers. I shared this with a wise older woman (the mother of four grown daughters), and she offered this wisdom: "No two children have the same set of parents. You need to accept that your life is constantly changing, and no two kids will have the exact same experience. Consider the gifts each child has because of their circumstances [in this case, Levi having three great older brothers, for example], and choose not to compare!" I've reminded myself of that wisdom many times since.

If you have more than one child, it's wise to recognize that each of your kids will have a unique personality, different circumstances, and, yes, even a different set of parents! With that in mind, keep character at the front of your mind in all seasons, and enjoy the uniqueness of all your children!

Character Training

I opened this chapter with the story of one of my sons going through a difficult season of lousy character. Jonah has grown up to have incredible character (and he's given me permission to share!), so I will reflect on his story here. While I was always aware and grateful that Jonah has never been openly rebellious—rude to his parents, using drugs, or rejecting his faith—we were dealing with the more subtle sins of having a critical nature and being argumentative and generally unpleasant to be around that made being his parent challenging.

Within a day of my exasperated beach scene, I had a seemingly random idea to try something new with Jonah. Realizing that he was growing up and knowing the power of role models and influences, I gathered a list of resources and a blank journal and then gave him a new daily assignment: in addition to his schoolwork, chores, and daily time with God, he was required to spend thirty minutes each morning watching, listening to, or reading something that would inspire good character. My list included YouTube channels, TED Talks, and a few podcasts and blogs. (I started with a simple list of things I knew of off the top of my head, so it wasn't a great list!) He could choose what to do each day, but he was required to journal the date, what resource he used, and at least one nugget he took away from it.

Jonah's initial response was frustration and resistance, but I didn't budge. He watched a video on the first day and couldn't deny it was encouraging. He journaled very little, but I kept reminding him of his task and checking his notes. After a few weeks I found his journal often had full pages of notes about what he'd taken in that day.

Soon I saw quotes or Bible verses on notecards hanging above Jonah's desk. Not overnight, but over time I witnessed this son reflecting more patience, kindness, and humility. He shared some of what he was learning, and along with continued Bible study, conversations, and discipline, I grew convinced that the character training exercise I'd assigned him was making a difference.

This son developed godly attributes as he recognized God's love for him and kindness to him. He was inspired by the great resources he was taking in. He also grew to understand the benefits of good character for his life both currently and in the future.

A Word to Dads

Character is a big topic, and Monica covered a lot in this chapter. My biggest dad advice is to simply be involved—to look for opportunities to talk to your kids about character, and, of course, to model it. And also realize that character development is one of the things where you need to take a long-game approach. It doesn't happen overnight, and it can be rough along the way.

Some of the character lessons we've taken our kids through were worked out in the confined space of our home. But it seems like some of the biggest lessons have occurred out in public where other parents were around to witness them. Oh joy.

Recently, I saw my youngest son let a bad shot get the best of him at a golf tournament where I was his caddy. He was doing fairly well until he took a few extra swings trying to get out of a bunker. With each extra swing, I saw the frustration on his face. Then in a burst of anger he threw his club onto the ground. It was a deep bunker, so maybe—hopefully—I was the only witness of this bad display of character.

He went on to finish with a fairly poor performance in the tournament.

This episode revealed to me an area I clearly need to work on with my son. After the tournament. I read in the rules that throwing clubs was an offense that could come with penalties and even losing the opportunity to play in future golf tournaments if it went far enough. My son and I had a long discussion about how managing emotions fits with the results we get in competition. We were

During his gap year between high school and college, Jonah created and hosted his own podcast called *The Truth for Youth Podcast*, where he interviewed inspiring role models, reviewed some of his favorite books, and highlighted the importance of character in a young person's life. You can imagine how happy I was when I considered his progress.

After sharing about my character training experiment in *Boy Mom*, many parents were interested in "character training" their own children. I spent the next summer pouring my heart into creating an online course that would help parents do exactly that. This online course now includes short modules covering the building blocks of good character in our kids and interviews with mothers and fathers who specialize on topics like sibling conflict, anger in parenting, helping kids find good friends and make good choices, and more.

There's also an extensive list of resources for the daily character training exercise, as well as a guide for how to implement it. In the resource section, you'll find a link to the Character Training Course information page.

Mom and Dad, your kids are amazing. But like mine, they're human. Every one of our kids will go through challenging stages, and part of our job is to help them and support them through it. We need extra-large doses of patience to raise these kids to be amazing adults. But even more, we must call our kids to a higher standard, one of excellent character.

If your heart aches to raise a child with noble character in this character-lacking world, I see you, and I want you to know I believe you can do it. Like my friend on the beach that New Year's Day, I'm nodding and smiling, cheering you on to keep believing, keep praying, and keep working on your child's character development.

also able to put those few bad strokes in a larger context and discuss how self-control goes way beyond results or scores in a golf tournament and will affect other areas over the course of his life.

As Monica and I have raised our kids, we've had numerous opportunities to discuss character in practical areas of life, like school, career, and just about anytime rules are involved. But even more, as parents we've also tried to go beyond external outcomes like grades or trophies. In our aim of "raising amazing" kids, we want them to have character that comes out of a heart that desires to please God. That begins with the profound knowledge that God created and loves them. As they put their faith and trust in who God is and the love he has for them, they develop a heart that finds its purpose in honoring and pleasing him.

It's a supernatural transformation that not only changes our attitude toward God but also those around us. There's really nothing greater for us to demonstrate who God is to our world than to display the Spirit-filled character described in Galatians 5:22–23. In this spiritual reality, the reason for character takes on eternal significance. And it goes beyond ourselves and can influence those around us. In fact, the greater parenting goal for Monica and me isn't to teach character to avoid a golf penalty or win a community service award; it's for our kids to live to glorify and please their Father in heaven and in doing so draw the world toward him!

This job of character building is a high calling, Dad. There's a good chance your wife is working hard at it, so step up your game and be a dad who's involved in shaping your kids' character. Not just when there's a penalty or public embarrassment, but in the everyday moments of life at home.

Thoughts from Josiah, Age Twenty-Two

Looking back at my childhood, I realize that my parents taught me about character in a lot of little, often hands-on ways. I remember my mom dragging us out the door on a Friday morning to get to the big gym across from the post office. We were on our way to help provide food for needy people in our community. I didn't think much of it at the time, but the ritual became a bedrock for how I think about my less-fortunate neighbors and find ways to love them.

After bagging up groceries and handing them out to the homeless and others in need, my brothers, my mom, and I would talk about what we did and why. This routine (and many others) contributed immensely to my character development, and now I realize that the activities and commitments my parents instilled in me as a boy shaped many of my perceptions and attitudes.

Without even realizing it my parents found ways to talk about and teach character through our daily activities, oftentimes the hard ones. When my brothers and I didn't get along, or I had a bad attitude, or I faced disappointment, the conversations that followed had less to do with the specific event and more to do with the character behind it.

Now I see what a privilege parents have to be given the ability and authority to contribute toward shaping their children's character.

Reflection Questions

1. Which area of character development is most on your mind with your child(ren) right now?

2. Which resource or approach to character development from this chapter do you imagine might be helpful to your family?

3. How would you describe your child's motivation to want to develop good, godly character? What kind of conversations do you think might inspire that motivation to grow?

CHAPTER 10

THE STRUGGLE IS REAL (AND ALSO GOOD)

Adversity Fuels Greatness

> *Show me someone who has done something worthwhile, and I'll show you someone who has overcome adversity.*
>
> —Lou Holtz

In my note at the beginning of the book, I said I'd tell the story of Jonah and the SAT test, so here it is:

During his junior year of high school, my son Jonah began to focus intently on his SAT test. He had a certain score in mind—what he thought he needed to be invited to a scholarship competition at Westmont College. His older brother, Josiah, had received the scholarship and was happy as a sophomore at Westmont. Jonah already had the grades, overall resumé, and a good chance at the scholarship, but exceptional SAT test scores were crucial.

The tricky thing was that standardized tests weren't Jonah's specialty. I tried to gently prepare him that Westmont might be out of reach. We weren't open to student loans, and our college savings weren't in the California-private-college range. I started highlighting the benefits of attending community college or our state university in Hawaii. Plenty of other options were out there if winning the scholarship didn't happen.

Jonah would have none of it.

He dove into every free SAT study guide he could find. From the College Board, Kahn Academy . . . You name it, he used it. He put himself on a study program and took countless practice exams. Finally, the day of his test arrived, and he walked out the door so confident that I wondered if he might just get a perfect score. Because if studying hard could get you a perfect score, then surely he had a chance.

Except, no. His test scores came back above average but not exceptional. My heart sank as I tried to figure out what he should do next.

Jonah didn't wait for me to tell him what to do next. He took only a minute to be disappointed before he enthusiastically dove back into studying, planning to test again the summer before his senior year of high school. He holed up at his desk for hours most days, studying and taking more practice exams. For each problem he got wrong, he wrote out what he did wrong by hand and what he might do differently next time. He read books with tips for outsmarting the SAT and joined online forums where students discussed each problem on the practice tests.

Jonah worked at a restaurant that summer, but otherwise he spent almost all his time studying. His brothers would joke saying, "Mom, this SAT studying is making Jonah crazy. We're not sure if he's even showering anymore!"

I had to agree he was in rare form. I prayed for wisdom, and while encouraging him to stay balanced (and to remember to shower), I tried to support his efforts.

Finally, the test day rolled around, and I was hesitantly optimistic. He walked out the door, and I dropped to my knees. It's funny how the hours can crawl by at times like these, but I will never forget his phone call from the parking lot after the test. Devastated, Jonah blurted, "I can't believe it, but I ran out of time on the math section! Math is what I usually do best on. I totally blew it." He choked on his words, and boy, did I feel his pain.

When the results came in, Jonah's concerns were confirmed: his score was hardly different from the first time. My husband and I talked about how we might redirect him to other options. That night I reminded Jonah of his great worth in Christ and urged him to pray about other options for college. He listened and said he'd sleep on it.

The next day Jonah emerged with the "great" news that he'd just calculated that if he took the SAT *one more time* that fall, his scores would come in just in time to be considered for the scholarship. I'm a little embarrassed to admit it, but I tried to talk him out of even signing up. "Usually scores just don't change that much," I said. *So much for a growth mindset, Mom.* "You've done your best. I think it's time to move on!"

But Jonah wasn't listening to me or anyone else. He paid for his own test and doubled down on his study efforts.

Weeks before the test Jonah asked me to set up a mock test for him. He was determined not to run out of time or be distracted on test day. He set up a fold-up desk in the living room and brought only a watch, a bottle of water, and his pencils. He asked me to act as proctor, pacing around and occasionally announcing the time. Dave thought we were crazy, but at this point I'd do anything to help.

Finally, for the third and last time, Jonah took the SAT test.

He drove home feeling much better than the time before. But we weren't going to hold our breath. Then two weeks later, days before his college application deadline (along with any hope for a scholarship) his test scores arrived.

Jonah's scores not only improved but were well within the range of what he needed to be invited to compete for the scholarship (insert all the emotions).

I'm happy to say that all of Jonah's dreams did come true after that, and as I write this he's finishing his sophomore year at Westmont. He's fitting in well and getting good grades as an engineering major. He belongs there, without a doubt. But, dang, he earned that scholarship and my respect.

Jonah's character grew moment by moment, disappointment by disappointment, failure by failure, as he would not give up. Winston Churchill once said, "Success consists of going from failure to failure without loss of enthusiasm." I think Churchill would have said Jonah had succeeded well before any test results came in.

Allow Adversity to Shape Your Kids

As much as I love reflecting on Jonah's SAT story, I'm aware that it's of the first-world type. Yet I love any good story of overcoming. In fact, though I can't seem to get my family to agree with me on what film to watch on movie nights—five boys against me?—one thing we all love is a good story of someone overcoming the odds to come out on top. Military movies, sports or survival stories, and just about any true story involving a good struggle with a focus on strong character will win over the Swanson family.

I've also loved reading biographies of great men and women of history with my boys. We've been inspired by incredible people who overcame great obstacles to do big things in the world. I want my boys to know, at least through the pages of books, that adversity isn't to be feared. By walking through the stories of others, I want them to shore up their confidence that when they encounter real-life challenges, they, too, might face them with courage, emerging even stronger.

Recently, Levi and I read the autobiography of Helen Keller, an American author, disability rights advocate, political activist, and lecturer, who was both blind and deaf from a young age. Keller said, "Character cannot be developed in ease and quiet. Only through experience of trial and suffering can the soul be strengthened, vision cleared, ambition inspired, and success achieved."[1]

While quarantined at home during the COVID-19 pandemic, the boys and I traveled through the pages of books to China with missionary Gladys Aylward, rode the underground railroad with abolitionist Harriet Tubman, and learned to navigate the open seas with mathematician Nathaniel Bowditch. We listened to the New Testament's apostle Paul tell tales of shipwrecks and beatings, being imprisoned for his faith, and how through all of this he learned to be content.

I'm overwhelmed with gratitude when I think of the great treasure these and many other stories are to my kids. Our children need to know—*they're empowered by knowing*—that, yes, life can be incredibly hard. Yet amazing men and women who have been through harder things than they're ever likely to face have survived and come out stronger. These stories are gifts to our children.

Good stories can light a spark of inspiration that will ignite into flames when they need it most.

Best or Worst

We must note something important about every great story of overcoming: the hero didn't become a hero just because they faced a challenge. In fact, what we don't see on big screens or read about in books are the countless people who faced challenges and did *not* rise up but instead gave up, the people who chose the path of fear, self-pity, or defeat. All of which, it turns out, is usually the path of least resistance. Perhaps it would be good if we heard more of these stories, because adversity can bring out our best or our worst. Ultimately, it's up to us.

The character we build in our daily lives is revealed when the pressure is on. Adversity has a way of drawing out character qualities that were previously less obvious. I once heard a pastor use a toothpaste tube analogy to describe character. He said like a tube of toothpaste, when we're "squeezed" (by adversity or stress of any kind), what comes out is what was in us all along.

I like The Message version of Jesus's words from Matthew 15:18: "What comes out of the mouth gets its start in the heart."

Bringing It Home

The truth is as much as my family loves to watch or read a good story full of challenge and overcoming, none of us enjoy challenge when it's our turn to face it. Just last night we gathered around the computer where my husband had found a TED Talk by a man speaking on the value of being uncomfortable. He shared his touching story of being fired from an important job, which made him face his deepest fears. Through his experience of feeling uncomfortable, he went on to discover his greatest success. The man displayed visual diagrams to show the importance of being in the "uncomfortable zone," and his enthusiasm captivated us.

"OK, boys, what uncomfortable thing are you ready to face?" Dave asked them.

"Surf bigger waves," Luke stated, unsurprisingly.

"I want to climb a mountain!" Levi piped in.

Inspiration was high. Then as Dave closed the laptop to put it away, I reminded Levi that it was his turn to do the dinner dishes. He moaned. "There are so many dishes. It's too hard."

Sometimes we'd rather climb a mountain than face a small mountain of dishes right in front of us.

I confess I like to be comfortable. I like hot showers and a soft bed. After years living in Hawaii, I can hardly stand to be in weather lower than 60 degrees. I don't like being hungry, being in pain, facing overwhelming tasks, or being criticized. (Tell me I'm not the only one.)

Even more than my own comfort, I want comfort for my kids in every way possible. I want them to be well fed and warm. I want them to be surrounded by nice people and to find success in everything they do. I want them to study hard but not so hard they lose sleep or experience stress. Honestly, if I *could* give my kids a pain-free, Bubble Wrap life, I probably would.

But that's not the path to greatness, is it?

I'd never suggest you seek out pain or hardship (I'd worry about you if you did), but at the same time, all evidence proves that difficult times in life build great character. So when adversity rears its scary head, the best thing we can do is face it, head-on.

But do we? Or as parents, do we make sure our kids do?

In an article in *Inc.* magazine, Jim Haudan wrote, "Unfortunately the most common response to adversity is to try and make it go away. The reality is that when you take away adversity you also take away one of the most important ingredients to greatness."[2]

Paul talks about the value of suffering in Romans 5:3–4: "We also glory in our sufferings, because we know that suffering produces perseverance; perseverance, character; and character, hope."

And hope is what we want for our kids, isn't it? We want to know that anytime our precious children experience suffering, it will ultimately lead to a deeper, more authentic hope in Jesus. In fact, to get from where our kids are today to where God wants them to be, some suffering will have to happen. And we as parents need to be OK with that.

If we shield our kids from all suffering, we might just be getting in the way of the good God is trying to produce in them.

> *If we shield our kids from all suffering, we might just be getting in the way of the good God is trying to produce in them.*

Importantly, while we love to read stories of war heroes or missionaries who have suffered and succeeded, we need to remember this plays out in our ordinary, everyday life as much as on the battlefield.

I like how C. S. Lewis said it: "Hardships often prepare ordinary people for an extraordinary destiny." I want my ordinary kids to have an extraordinary destiny, and I bet you do too.

Getting Practical

You might sense my elevated heart rate as I write about this topic. But the important thing for us as parents is this: how this view of adversity should impact our parenting. Let's dive in.

Some of Our Kids Are Facing Hard Stuff

Some of you are raising kids who live with adversity every day. Perhaps they have physical, emotional, mental, or learning challenges. Some of them have been or will be bullied. You may be a parent (perhaps single), a grandparent, or a foster parent raising a child who deals with wounds you wish they never had to face. Your child may struggle to concentrate, kick a ball, do math, or make friends. You might have kids who will one day fail a test upon which their dreams depend, get their heart broken, or receive an awful diagnosis. (I might too.) A lot of life is hard.

In these times, adversity can make a person bitter, or it can make them better. The choice is up to each of us. And our job, our privilege, and our responsibility as parents is to make sure our kids know this well. If your child faces real challenges in life, he or she needs parents who love and support them. They need empathy and coaching. If you can listen, care, and walk them through their hardest days, you show them God's love in the most important way.

But know that our kids will be empowered if we teach them to face their challenges bravely and to become stronger through them. Even as our kids face difficulties, we can cheer them on to be courageous. We can help them choose integrity, hard work, and faith. Our kids need to know they're not victims of their circumstances. They will also benefit from learning young that they can find great blessings even in times of suffering. James 1:2–4 is an important Scripture passage to know and teach: "Consider it pure joy, my brothers and sisters, whenever you face trials of many kinds, because you know that the testing of your faith produces perseverance. Let perseverance finish its work so that you may be mature and complete, not lacking anything."

Our kids are blessed by knowing that God can use any and every trial they go through for his glory and their good. My friend Nicole has a daughter, Faith, who was born with damage to her arm, leading to amputation just below the elbow. Faith grew up passionate about the ocean and wanting to surf. Her mom said she always told her daughter she could do anything with one hand that most people do with two. So rather than dissuade her from surfing, Nicole cheered her on. In time Faith began traveling to compete in surf contests all over the world. She has become a role model for other young girls who are also overcoming personal obstacles.

The story of Joseph in Genesis is one of my favorites. After years of abandonment by his brothers and mistreatment and misunderstanding by others, eventually the tables turned when he was promoted to a place of great power. Soon after, his brothers came to him in desperate need of help. If you haven't read the story, I highly recommend reading it start to finish (Genesis 37–50), but my favorite verse comes at the end when Joseph could say to his brothers, "You intended to harm me, but God intended it for good" (Gen. 50:20).

If your child is in a difficult season, I am so sorry. Nothing pierces a parent's heart like seeing their child in pain. My good friend who's a family therapist and a widowed mom to two teenagers suggests that kids who are hurting most need a parent who is consistently there to empathize, encourage, and explore ways to make things better.

Faith's mom, Nicole, said this was true for her. In fact, she recalls a great moment of relief after confessing to a pastor that she and Faith were both struggling to accept her arm amputation. He reminded her that we live in a fallen world and there will be pain and suffering, and he said it's OK to just say it's miserable sometimes and be sad. But in doing so, we can also bring our hurts to God, who will be near us in our painful times and walk with us through them.

Though sometimes it seems like there's nothing we can do, we can always pray. We can always point our kids to God, who knows all and loves them deeply. We can speak words of life and truth, even when we personally struggle to believe them. This is parenting through true adversity. And though it may be the hardest thing you ever do, it may be one of the most holy.

In the midst of adversity, let's make sure to parent our kids to this end: "We know that in all things God works for the good of those who love him" (Rom. 8:28).

Now, Let's Be Honest

Some of you might be having a moment of truth, thinking, "Whoa. My child hasn't faced much adversity." Perhaps they're healthy, well liked, and doing OK in school. I get it. The fact is most of our kids have relatively easy lives. They're fed three meals a day (plus snacks!), they sleep in a bed, and they're loved by their parents. And we wouldn't want it any other way, would we?

I love giving my kids a comfortable life as much as anyone, but I've studied this stuff enough now to know that kids with easy lives will face some disadvantages when they get out into the world. We're not doing them any favors by giving them a soft, comfortable life (dang!).

So the question is this: If adversity is fuel for greatness, and our kids don't have much true adversity in their lives, what are we supposed to do? Well, hold on to your Bubble Wrap while I say the next thing.

We may need to create challenges for our kids. It's our responsibility as parents to build our kids' character muscles— their work ethic, patience, grit, and integrity—while we're raising them. Because as comfy as our kids might be today, they will face difficult times eventually. And it's up to you and me, Mom and Dad, to make sure they're prepared.

It's our responsibility as parents to build our kids' character muscles.

How to Challenge Our Comfortable Kids

I'm a big believer in talking to our kids about adversity before they face it. Teach them to expect it and empower them by saying you believe they have what it takes to face it. I love Tom Hanks's line in the film *A League of Their Own*: "It's supposed to be hard. If it were easy, everyone would do it."

The truth is, adversity is not always blood and guts or a story worthy of a documentary on the Discovery Channel. In my home, anyway, daily so-called adversities often come in the form of difficult math problems, being told no to more screen time, or taking out the trash, yet again!

I'm often tempted to help my son finish his math assignment or let him get by with doing a shoddy job on chores. But deep down I know I can do better than that. Our goal should never be to win our children's friendship or make sure they experience happiness every moment of their childhood. Our job is to train them up to be amazing humans. So, before you go looking for a mountain for your child to climb, start at home, training them to be humble and kind. To face challenges with courage. And yes, to take out that trash with dignity.

QUIT RESCUING THEM

Your child might face daily challenges, but you don't recognize them because you're so busy *managing those challenges for them.* If you simply quit shielding your child from difficult times, they might grow up with more grit and grace. Let them finish their own science project or get the grade they deserve if they don't. Let them talk to their teacher about an issue before you call and get involved. When they forget their lunch for the tenth time, you might even (don't gasp) let them go hungry that day! I'm not kidding; they won't die.

MAKE THEM WORK

Your child can begin doing chores at an early age. When they're young it usually creates more work for the parents than for the kids, but it's still worthwhile to train them. My boys have a rotating chore system that relieves me of a lot of household work. In addition, we offer them extra jobs for pay as they grow up, inside the house or in the yard.

There are many chore systems you might choose from, (and ways to include payment, or not) or you might create your own approach. In the resources section, you'll find a link to the chore system I created after years of frustration, as well as a "Life Skills by Age" sheet, which can offer a general idea for what typical children ought to be capable of by various ages. But whatever you use, I highly recommend setting a high standard of work ethic in your home. This was at one time usual and assumed in American life. (Think milking cows at 4:00 a.m., weeding a massive family garden, or tending to outhouse duties. None of that was so long ago, and some of those chores are still typical for children in parts of the world.)

I've found that even the most reluctant kids find a certain satisfaction with a job well done. There's pride in accomplishing a difficult task (yes, *difficult* is a relative term). And having kids work together is great for sibling relationships, even if it takes a while to get there.

A child who learns to be a good worker will likely become a happier, more well-adjusted child. I've seen more than one youngster in my home shift from a foul mood to a proud disposition when left alone in the kitchen with a pile of dishes, some good music, and a family trusting him to make plates and glasses sparkle.

Our boys secured internships in early high school and got real jobs when they earned their driver's license. Kids can also pick up work from friends or neighbors. There are more and more online options for work if transportation is an issue. It may take some creativity, but I think we can all agree: Children benefit from work. Especially when it's hard. This is one area worth being intentional about.

TEACH THEM TO DO HARD THINGS

Every time one of our boys complains about something they have to do, my husband and I remind them of one of our family mottos: "Swansons do hard things." Your kids can learn to play an instrument, build a challenging Lego set (or a piece of furniture!), try a new hobby, or make their own bed. (If you have bunk beds, then fitted sheets qualify as a hard thing.) My husband and I regularly put challenging things on our kids' plates, and it keeps them busy and out of trouble. We also expect them to take difficult classes and get good grades. If they're challenged, we'll help them figure out the problem, but we certainly don't let them give up too quickly.

Team sports or any activity that requires your child to learn from an adult other than their own parents and work alongside others is great for character building. Look for opportunities to challenge your kids, then step back and let them struggle. They might throw a little fit (and if this is new to them, expect that), but when they're done, you better believe you'll spot a look of satisfaction on their faces. Cheer them on and celebrate their efforts. When a family embraces a "do hard things" mentality, kids rise up. And in time they are likely to be noticed for this increasingly rare quality.

Raising kids to embrace adversity may be challenging at times, but I truly believe it's worth it. As Jim Haudan wraps up his thought, "In simple terms: no adversity, no growth. Instead of avoiding adversity, we need to hug it! It is the fuel for greatness."[3]

A Word to Dads

Dad, you certainly have a big job being a protector and provider. Your family needs the strength and security that's unique to having a father in the house. You're there to make life better and in many ways easier for your kids.

It's in a father's heart to be that way. A dad will do whatever is necessary to make sure his kids have a roof over their heads and food on the table.

But our kids will eventually need the skills to navigate the world and its challenges themselves. The day they have to jump out of the nest is coming. Before it happens, though, they need a chance to flap and exercise those wings through introductions to things like hard work, sacrificing their time for others, and learning the ropes of household and outdoor chores.

Helping your kids value what they have is a good starting point. They need to know that, in general, as far as the material world is concerned, nothing is for free. Someone had to pay for that delicious ice cream in the freezer. It had to be paid for with money someone earned. As time goes by, one of your roles as a dad is to help your kids understand this.

Doing hard work is where those good things often come from. Kids need to sometimes work before play and be taught the principle of delayed gratification. You can find age-appropriate ways to teach these principles over time. Don't be afraid to ask your kids to help. Give them opportunities to make and save and give money. Look for opportunities in the community as well.

When our oldest son was twelve, he really wanted a new surfboard. A local surfboard shaper shared our passion for helping kids understand the value of work. He let Josiah clean up in his shop a few days a week during a semester of school and kept track of his hours until he'd worked enough to earn the price of a new surfboard. This was much better than Josiah waiting on his parents to save our money to buy him one as a gift. He got a board plus the knowledge of the value behind it—his hard work. Needless to say, he appreciated and took good care of it.

Challenges will be part of your kid's life experience in relationships as well. The world is a hard place, and as soon as your kids step out the door, they'll be confronted with this fact. Your job will be to help them navigate those challenges so one day they'll be able to do it on their own.

I remember the day one of my sons came home from a youth group event in tears over having been bullied. I had to decide how to help him navigate the situation. I could call the kid's dad (I knew him), he could stay home the next time and avoid future situations with the other kid, or he could work on a strategy to help him manage both his feelings and the situation in a constructive way.

Together, we chose the final option. I helped him work through some of his feelings, and he was able to get perspective on the situation. I also coached him on a strategy for future encounters. It didn't involve an MMA coach, but it did involve giving him advice on what to say and how to react in a way that would put responsibility on the other kid.

The world won't be easy on your kids, so keeping them in a bubble won't be doing them any favors. I've often had a hard time with wanting to protect my kids or rescue them from struggles even though I know they need to experience them. I want them to be happy. But I know that, ultimately, I need to trust God more than I trust my feelings. As a parent, I need to tap into God's ability to provide for my kids' needs in challenges they face that he will ultimately use to shape them into who he wants them to be.

Thoughts from Luke, Age Eighteen

I think adversity is one of the greatest keys to success: not only as an athlete but as a human being as well. As a competitive surfer, I've lost a lot more than I've won. I believe losing provides a great opportunity for growth, an opportunity I sure don't want to miss. Because loss comes so often as an athlete, I've been able to practice learning from it instead of complaining and making excuses. Every time I lose, instead of just letting me bask in the dreadfulness of it, my parents ask me whether there is something to learn about myself that could help me get better (and there is always something). That being said, when I choose to trust God and accept adversity, I definitely grow the most. I believe God has wired us in a spectacular way, that when we trust in him completely, we can find the strength to overcome our adversities and be unstoppable.

Reflection Questions

1. What are some hard things your child is facing?

2. What are some ways you might inspire your child to recognize the importance of doing hard things in order to grow?

3. Where might you offer some challenges or work responsibilities to help your child develop greater character?

CHAPTER 11

HELP SIBLINGS BECOME FRIENDS

*Cultivate Connections
That Last a Lifetime*

*Behold, how good and pleasant it is
when brothers dwell in unity!*
—**Psalm 133:1 ESV**

The phone rang while I was making dinner. With two sons in college on the west coast of California, it seems their "wind down and call Mom" time often hits just as I'm bustling to prepare food for the four of us at home. But I love hearing their voices, and this evening I picked up the phone while slowly stirring a pot of soup.

Josiah sounded especially happy—not with news about grades or interest in a girl but with what might sound like a strange announcement: "Mom, I just have to tell you, I'm so glad Jonah came to college here! We are seriously best friends."

I smiled to myself, curious to know what inspired his enthusiasm.

He went on. "I just realized I haven't told you how much I love having my brother at college with me. I mean, I honestly wasn't sure what it would be like with him here this year. You know how different we are."

I nodded at the understatement.

Josiah continued, "When he first started, I was so tempted to tell him what to do—to coach him to find the right friends and everything else. But I made myself stand back and let him have his own experience. And now I'm watching him just crush college life, and I'm actually learning a lot from him. He's seriously the best brother, and he's my best friend."

A few happy tears might have been mixed into the soup that night.

The truth is my college boys *are* best friends, but they also consider themselves best friends with their two younger brothers still at home. Luke, eighteen, talks to one of his two college brothers a few times a week, and they're constantly sending text messages, Instagram memes, and other hilarity back and forth. Levi, twelve (six and a half years younger than Luke), is also in the mix—and not just as a courtesy. His brothers include him generously in as much as they can when they're home and keep in conversation with him while they're away.

It's incredibly special seeing these friendships grow along with my boys. So I have pondered and been asked this question a lot: How did this happen? How did my boys grow up to be best friends?

I'll share the things I believe have contributed to their strong relationships, but first, let me be clear that my boys are not unicorns. Those same four sons have squabbled, rivaled, and all-out battled at various points. They've wrestled until they broke Lego sets, furniture, and even Jonah's right arm. (Big brother claims they were "play wrestling," but the jury is still out.) I've had to break up fights, wipe tears, coach, and counsel each of them on many occasions. Everyone in our family is human, and we'll never claim to have perfect relationships.

It's also important to note that not all siblings can be, or *need* to be, best friends. Most of us will be happy if our kids like each other and get along, especially if we all hope to gather as adults for holidays and in times of celebration or need. But I think it's worthwhile to parent with the intention of helping our kids develop strong connections. And if they end up best friends along the way (now or later)? That's a bonus.

Does It Really Matter If Our Kids Become Close?

In the weariness of day-to-day parenting, many moms and dads throw in the towel when it comes to trying to get their kids to be friends. "I always dreamed that my kids would be great friends, but my son and daughter just can't stand each other," one mom told me. Then she added with a shrug, "They've only got two more years before my oldest goes to college, so we'll make it through. And who knows—maybe they'll become friends later in life!"

I've also heard from parents who are just keeping the peace by making sure their kids are staying busy and out of each other's way. "As long as they have friends to play with and separate activities, they do OK!" another mom said.

This approach might work for some families, at least in the short-term. But when the world began lockdowns due to COVID-19, suddenly it wasn't so easy to avoid one another. Many families faced a scary predicament: *a ton of time together and no escape.* The pandemic brought a lot of issues to the surface, and the effect on sibling relationships varied greatly—from brothers and sisters whose relationship went from bad to worse, to those who, in the midst of the lockdown, discovered a friendship they would otherwise have missed.

But the question remains, If our kids simply tolerate one another, is that good enough?

According to the research, sibling relationships do matter, and they matter for a lifetime. The nature of sibling relationships in childhood echo for the rest of our lives. An article published in the *American Journal of Psychiatry* suggests that the quality of sibling relationships is one of the most important predictors of mental health into old age.[1] Additional research shows that people who are emotionally connected to their siblings have higher life satisfaction and lower rates of depression later in their lives.[2]

Many studies also suggest we not wait for the magic to happen in adulthood. Geoffrey Greif, a professor at the University of Maryland School of Social Work and coauthor of *Adult Sibling Relationships*, wrote that how siblings get along as children is indicative of how they'll get along as adults. He looked at case studies consisting of more than 260 siblings above the age of forty and found that children who had poor relationships with their siblings were more likely to continue a negative relationship into adulthood.

"You're better off having a good relationship when you're young, so you don't have to learn how to do it when you're older," Greig said in a recent interview. "And if you have it when you're young and you get into trouble when you're old, then you've got a better history to fall back on."[3]

So, yes, it's worth putting some serious effort into helping our kids develop strong connections with their siblings as they're growing up. There are no guarantees, and even with the best parental intentions, things don't always go as we hope. But if we as parents are purposeful, we can feel good knowing we did our best to foster healthy relationships among our children.

If you hope your kids will grow up to be well connected, or maybe even good friends, the best advice I have is to make them spend plenty of time together. It won't always be easy, but in the end, time together is what bonds people.

Here are a few simple ways to set up your kids for sibling success.

Provide Time for Your Kids to Play Together

Playdates with friends are great, but when we plan too many of them, kids don't learn to get along with their own siblings. Most of my boys' early years were spent at home, at the park, or running errands all with their brothers and me. Yes, those were some long days, but looking back, I believe a lot of bonding happened. When kids are bored and have only each other, you'd be surprised by how creative they can get. Before you know it the siblings who couldn't stand each other ten minutes ago are teaming up to build a fort, defeat a bad guy, or hunt for a lost treasure (likely in the kitchen, under your feet!).

Depending on personalities, a lot of kids will ask to have friends over or go to a friend's home, but I suggest reserving those visits for "sometimes," not every day.

Vacation Just as a Family

I know a lot of people love to vacation with other families or bring a friend or two on their own family vacay. That's super cool, and it can be a lot of fun. *Sometimes*. I suggest that most of the time when you get away as a family you make it just your family. Road trips are an excellent time for sibling bonding and to help focus on character. When we're cooped up together is when the good stuff happens. Issues are worked out, and memories are made.

Have Your Kids Share a Bedroom . . . and Maybe a Car

I think sharing bedrooms is one of the best ways to foster lifelong connections between your kids. If you have the space and want to give each of your kids their own room, that can be awesome. But we chose to bunk our boys two to a room even while we had an extra room. If you do this, sure, your kids might get irritated, but in the end they'll learn skills to help them get along with a college roommate or an eventual spouse.

They'll also learn to compromise on space, schedules, and noise levels, and they'll often end up talking about life simply because they're in there together. I used to love hearing my oldest boys talk late into the night in their teenage years. I believe what happened there was knitting their lives together for the kind of friendship they now enjoy as young adults.

As kids get older, life gets more complicated, but that means you can find even more ways to teach them to cooperate. If you're blessed to have an extra car a young driver can use, it's good to let siblings know it will be shared. Have the older sibling give their younger siblings rides when they can, and have them all care for the car together, knowing that one day the younger siblings will be using it as well.

A Home(school) Advantage

We homeschool our children, and homeschooling can give families an advantage in the sibling bonding department. When my sons were young, they took many subjects together, our adjusting the curriculum according to age. As they got older, they worked with more independent curriculum, which put them on separate computers in various areas of the house. Still, they interacted throughout the day. They talked over breaks, went outside to toss a ball or skateboard, ate lunch together, and sometimes even helped one another with schoolwork (Mom's favorite, especially when it's calculus!).

Homeschooling doesn't guarantee kids will bond or even spend time together. Some students might do their work independently, then dash out the door to work, play a sport, or hang out with friends. And if you allow kids to spend time on devices during break times, that can easily replace time connecting with siblings (or anything else, really). But the fact that your home is quite literally *home base* for all things school means you have the opportunity to cultivate strong sibling connections.

For those who highly value sibling connections *and* have the desire to try homeschooling, this may be a strong reason to try it.

Give Your Kids Some Space

Luke has shared a room with Levi since Levi was born, and they're very close. So close, in fact, that sometimes Dave and I feel Levi connects with Luke as though his brother is a parent. He's often attached to Luke Velcro-style, and Luke has been a trooper, allowing it all these years.

But now Luke, eighteen to his brother's twelve, could use a bit (OK, a whole lot) more privacy and freedom. So as I write this, he's recently moved into his own bedroom. It's been so fun seeing Luke flourish in his own space, and interestingly, Levi flourishing in his.

We'll never get the balance perfect (in anything, right?), but kids do need downtime, quiet, and space, especially as they get older. While I always encourage families to keep their kids close, I also recommend paying attention to the unique personalities and temperaments of every family member. Time apart, alone time individually with Mom and Dad, and playtime with kids their own age are all important parts of the big picture. Our hope is that after some time apart, siblings will come back together to appreciate each other even more.

Sibling Role Models for the Win

If you asked my boys what helped them grow up to be so close, I guarantee they would all mention a few inspiring examples they've seen in other families—siblings a few years ahead of them in life.

Our friends the Hulse family in San Clemente, California, are a good example. Pastor George and his wife, Cheryl, have two sons and a daughter. Their kids attended public high school but grew up very close. They all three went on to attend Point Loma College in San Diego, and they often share posts on social media of the siblings hanging out together like best friends. On their birthdays or for special occasions, they post super kind captions about one another. Seeing that sibling affection planted a seed in my boys' minds.

We can all point our kids to great examples of healthy sibling relationships in books or in movies, in real life or online. It may take some creativity, but I encourage you to help your kids find them.

Involve Your Kids in the Same Extracurriculars

I spent time talking to Brooklyn, the youngest of the three Hulse siblings, and asked her what she thought might have been the key to their strong sibling friendship. One thing she mentioned was the fact that they often played sports together. "My parents didn't want to be running all over from the beach to tennis to track, so they told us whatever one of us did each season we all had to do!"

I laughed at the practicality of that idea.

"Seriously," Brooklyn told me. "One year I didn't make the Junior Lifeguard program, so my mom pulled my brothers out! She said, 'Fine, then. You'll all play tennis this summer!'"

Now the three of them surf and play tennis and do just about everything together, and they continue to inspire my sons.

I've heard of some families who allow one child to choose a sport or activity per season, and the others either join the same one or sit that season out and support their siblings. This is a great idea, especially for the younger years.

The reality is signing kids up for the same activity isn't always easy, nor is it always best. You may have a talented musician in your family as well as a gifted dancer and another who loves wrestling. This is all good, and it's important to celebrate our kids' uniqueness. Yet I do think it's worth considering when and where we might simplify life in this way. Especially when kids are young, we can introduce them to the same activities and then see what pans out over time.

Foster Your Kids Working as a Team

Teamwork works. Working side by side is truly a bonding experience. I highly recommend giving your kids chores that require teamwork to complete. My boys' chore system is set up so each one has a zone of the house to cover on his own, but his chores all depend on the others doing their part. I also assign them side jobs they must do together, such as washing the cars, organizing the garage, or doing yard work. My boys have also picked up jobs from other families together, which means they're not only working side by side but eyes are often on them while they work.

My friend Krista Gilbert has one daughter and three sons. Her daughter, McKenna, spent a couple of nights with us while she was studying in Hawaii last winter, and I got to ask her a bunch of questions about her family (my favorite thing to do!). From Krista's book *Reclaiming Home*, it was clear to me that they were a tight-knit family, and I was curious to hear from one of the children.

McKenna said her parents were intentional about family time. "Dinners were a big deal. We all ate together whenever possible, and no devices were allowed at the table. My parents were really intentional about the conversations, and meals were a serious bonding time."

Then McKenna told me more about their evening routine. After dinner, the Gilbert parents excused themselves to another room for "couch time" so they could catch up on their day and relax. The kids were all expected to team up to clean and do the dishes, and everything had to be spotless when their parents returned.

I had to ask, "And what if it wasn't spotless?"

McKenna laughed. "I have no idea! We would never have tested that!"

I knew I loved Krista.

But Seriously, Have Fun!

Shared positive experiences are some of the greatest building blocks of any relationship. On a boring day, my youngest son will replay, out loud, every moment he can recall of a trip we took to my parents' cabin in Washington State. He talks about all the fun "the brothers" had, building a campfire, finding rocks in the river, throwing snowballs, and playing cards late into the night. What he doesn't remember (but I do) is the multiple arguments and bickering that went on during that trip. In Levi's memory it was all good.

I'm a huge fan of taking kids on trips. And if you ask my boys, they'll say that the simpler and more rustic they are, the better! But if travel isn't possible, then at least try to plan experiences your kids will remember, like family hikes, campouts in the yard or living room, or a spontaneous run for ice cream after dinner.

I asked Luke for his number one piece of advice for raising

siblings to be close friends, and he said, "Shared adventures!" I believe the shared adventures my boys took in their imaginations count. After years of playing a game they literally called "Imagination" in our backyard, my oldest son wrote and published his book *Sub-Marine*, which chronicles the stories they used to explore together.

This is another reminder of why it's important to get kids off screens and devices and into their imaginations. You never know what they might come up with, *especially together.*

Finally, A Little Dose of ~~Brainwashing~~ Encouragement

It may seem kids aren't really listening to us, but I've grown convinced they hear more than we think. When kids are young, we can speak life into their relationships by focusing on the beauty and value of their special sibling connection. Simply mentioning—and often—things like, "What a blessing that you have a little sister to teach so many things!" and "Wow, you're lucky to have a big brother who looks out for you!" might do more than you would think.

Let your kids know that family is for a lifetime, and while friends may come and go, siblings will always be there. Require them to treat each other with appreciation and respect—and be prepared with consequences if they don't. Remind them how well they treat their friends and neighbors and require them to treat their siblings with the same thoughtfulness. Notice when they're kind or helpful to their siblings, and praise them for that behavior.

Let your kids know that family is for a lifetime, and while friends may come and go, siblings will always be there.

I won't pretend that any of this is easy. But if your kids currently fight like crazy or avoid one another's company, don't assume that will always be the case. My boys have gone through stages like that, and while we didn't like it, we gave them space for a season. I believe this enabled them to then "choose" their siblings with their free will. Like all of us, kids need permission to choose.

And if they choose not to be friends, there's still plenty of hope that their relationship will change in later years. I'm much closer to my older brothers now than I was growing up!

It does take work to raise amazing kids. But when our tendency is to tune out or farm the kids out, it might just be time to lean in and double up on our efforts. Perhaps you, like me, need to write Galatians 6:9 on a posterboard in your closet: "Let us not become weary in doing good, for at the proper time we will reap a harvest if we do not give up."

Take a moment to imagine your kids as young adults hanging out together—because they want to be together! Let that image and idea fuel your efforts to get intentional about cultivating that sibling bond.

Note: Because sibling conflict is a big concern for parents, I wrote a bonus chapter, "Good and Pleasant: A Guide for Conflict Resolution and Peacemaking between Siblings." You can find a link to it in the resource section.

A Word to Dads

If you have more than one child, you've learned how tough it can be for you and your wife to juggle diaper changes and get through mealtime. Kids will work you, and it seems like you can never be totally on top of it. Then when you take the *them versus you* and add the *them versus them,* you've got to take off your opposing team jersey and put on the referee's.

A loud whistle will probably help too. As your kids start growing up, the competition can heat up. Kids arguing and fighting with each other can take over what was once a peaceful home. Conflict resolution is a real thing, and more likely than not you'll need to be the one brokering a peace deal.

Monica tells me that sibling conflict is one of the things she hears from parents most about. So, dads, this may be an opportunity to lean into and bless your wife. You're the dad, and your disciplining and peacemaking skills may be more effective than you realize. Get involved in the conversation with your kids. Give them some coaching. Help create a neutral zone for communication to happen. Maintain order in the court. Help guide conversations so they're fair and respectful. You might offer some rewards for peacefully coexisting—a game night or weekend outing if siblings put effort into sharing, getting along, or ending a fight before it starts. If you leave the home for work, be sure they know you'll be checking in to see how they do, and then be sure to do it. Your wife will appreciate the support, and kids are likely to rise up a little extra to make Dad proud.

Thoughts from Levi, Age Twelve

The best part of my growing up has been time with my brothers. I'm a lot younger than they are, so sometimes I've felt jealous that they had a lot of years together without me. But I have to admit they've been really nice to make me feel like I'm one of them. They take me places a lot—to their youth events or bonfires at the beach or even on road trips camping.

I do almost everything they do, which my mom tells me isn't normal. But if I could, I would tell all the older siblings out there that this is one of the nicest things you can do for your little brother or sister. Include them in things, and they will appreciate it so much.

My big brothers have set a great example for me in many ways. They teach me about good music and surfing, and most of all they talk a lot about their relationship with God. They read the Bible with me and make me want to be more like Jesus. They also laugh at my jokes.

I'm so glad I have siblings.

Reflection Questions

1. If you have more than one child, what is your greatest challenge in their current relationship?

2. How much time do your kids spend together in a typical day? Is there a way you might foster more quality (and perhaps quantity) time between them?

3. How would you like to see your kids getting along as they enter their older teen and adult years? Consider talking to them about their future and helping them recognize the value of working on developing a good friendship now.

CHAPTER 12

HOW THEY SPEND THEIR DAYS

Navigate School, Sports, Hobbies, and Free Time

> *How we spend our days is, of course, how we spend our lives.*
>
> **—Annie Dillard**

As my oldest sons have launched into greater independence, one of the many and sometimes tear-filled realizations I've had is how valuable and fleeting the ordinary days are. My heart aches a little trying to remember what it was like to wake up to little boys with sippy cups and Curious George on a weekday morning or sitting at a dinner table with two kids in braces. I want to better remember listening to each of them struggle through their first "I Can Read It!" books or watching them awkwardly kick a soccer ball, sometimes into their own goal.

I have plenty of photos of the highlights—birthday parties and Christmas mornings—but not many of the more typical daily scenes of kids hunkered over a pile of Legos or eating another bowl of Cheerios in their blue-striped PJs. (I'm grateful I can still see them in my memory.)

But now that most of my boys are grown, I can adapt Annie Dillard's observation: how they spent their young days pretty well sums up how they spent their childhood as a whole. They're not so much a product of the big, peak moments but of the everyday rituals: the dependable though not at all fancy meals, and chores, and rules, and routines, and books and baths and bedtime prayers. These are the things that have shaped their lives and were part of the story that traveled with them to college and will go with them beyond.

If I were to sit with you over coffee, I would encourage you to take a deep breath, whatever stage your kids are in, and consider the ordinary days. I would tell you that while God's grace is abundant, and I'm thankful I have few big regrets, if I could go back and do it again (pausing to wipe tears I imagine dripping into my coffee but are actually falling onto my keyboard), I would have soaked more in the daily things.

I would have made choices based less on what I thought I *needed* to do and more on what would bring the boys the most joy and wonder. I'd plan my sons' days less around what other moms are doing (I can be a victim of FOMO) and more around the things that light my boys up. I probably would trade some home project expenses for a few more family adventures. We'd eat more dinners on a blanket in the yard, and I would definitely lean in to listen to more of their rambling stories and not just pretend to.

There is no doubt parents (OK, especially us moms) have a tendency to reminisce and get sentimental like this. It is a bittersweet pastime I catch myself doing more each year. But there's a reason I mention these reflections here: I want to remind all of us who still have kids to raise to consider these things *while we're still in the raising*. We have this opportunity to make choices—choices to do the big and small things that will one day be the lifetime memories.

The Early Years

When kids are young, they're completely dependent on us. They don't know the difference between a good use of their time and a waste of their time. They don't know that exercise is healthy, or that music is enriching, or that reading will pay off later, or that too much screen time is bad for their brain. Sure, they'll discover those things one day, but until they're mature and wise enough to figure them out, it's *all on us* to lead them. (Yikes, right?) While I don't want to put too much pressure on us as parents, there's no denying that we're the ones who will determine, by choice or by default, how kids spend their time when they're young.

Ouch. I felt that one deep in my gut.

This idea can be overwhelming, but I'm not trying to freak you out. So let me insert right here that a whole lot of your kids' childhoods will happen naturally. God knows all the details of your life—where you live, what's available to your family, and all the others. You won't mess up his ultimate plans for your kids' lives, so let's not even go there. Deep breaths. It's all going to be OK!

Yet (you knew it was coming, right?) there *is* a lot you can do to give your kids the best childhood possible. It's worth taking the time to make some good choices now. So just as if we were indeed having coffee, I want to next take a brief look at some of the most important ways kids spend their childhood—with some considerations for each one.

School

One of the most significant shaping factors in your child's life will be their educational experience. By the time children graduate from high school, a traditionally schooled child will have spent fourteen thousand hours in school classrooms. *Fourteen. Thousand. Hours!* That's more of a child's waking hours than they'll spend at home or anywhere else.

Those fourteen thousand hours include a child's academic education but much more. Spending eight hours a day, five days a week (approximately thirty-five weeks a year) in school will undeniably shape their character, their convictions, and their understanding of the world. The curriculum used in the classroom will impact their worldview. The classmates they spend time with will influence who they're becoming. And, obviously, the teachers your child sits under will impact them for better or worse.

If we worry about how much time our kids spend on games or social media, we should be as concerned about the hours they spend in a school setting.

So if we worry about how much time our kids spend on games or social media, we should be as concerned about the hours they spend in a school setting.

Before I had kids, I would never have imagined being a homeschool parent. But we decided to "give it a try" when our oldest was in second grade, and we never turned back. Initially, I was hesitant (OK, scared to death) and my husband was skeptical ("Aren't homeschoolers kind of weird?"). But now that, as I write this chapter, we've graduated not two but three boys from homeschooling (and the first two earned college scholarships), I can say without any hesitation that homeschooling our boys was one of the most wonderful, pivotal parts of their lives. *And ours.* We wouldn't trade that part of our story for anything.

Since my first two boys have launched, I've explored more about the general direction public schools are heading, and my enthusiasm for homeschooling has only grown. I know I'm not alone in this.

A U.S. Census Bureau analysis report dated March 22, 2021, revealed that although homeschooling had remained steady at 3.3 percent since 2012 after growing rapidly since 1999, more growth took place starting in 2020: "By fall, 11.1% of households with school-age children reported homeschooling (Sept. 30–Oct. 12)."[1]

Yes, some of those homeschooling decisions were prompted by the COVID-19 pandemic, but more families are pulling kids from public schools to try homeschooling all the time. Though they've decided to homeschool for many reasons, for Christian families, there's a valid concern over cultural trends that have become normalized in many public schools.

I know homeschooling isn't the only option, and in some cases it's not the best option. Some private schools are doing their best to offer a genuine, Christ-centered environment for students, and if that's an option for you, it's worth considering. They often have scholarships available as well, which is a good thing. They can be pricey.

But I suggest that if you're a sincere Christ follower, and you have the *ability* to homeschool (even if it takes some schedule rearranging, sacrifice, or a complete downsize-compromise on your lifestyle), it's worth some prayerful consideration. You might just surprise yourself like I did and end up loving it! (Not every day, but the general experience.)

If you're a Christian and choose to send your kids to public school, I encourage you to prepare them to approach the experience with a missionary mindset: Find out as much as you can about the principal, the teachers, and how you might be able to be involved in the school. Talk to your children about what they'll be learning and prepare them for the variety of kids and viewpoints they'll be confronted with. (Chapter 14 will help with this.)

Without a doubt, what you do at home is the most important thing. No matter where your kids go to school, a God-centered, healthy, happy home will be the foundation that shapes them the most. If your kids go to school outside of the home, take time to pray for them each day and touch base every evening. Have open dialogue about what's being taught so your kids know you can help them navigate when evolution or sex-ed or gender issues come up. If you begin your days with the Bible and prayer and spend evenings discussing their day in light of a biblical worldview, and if they have a supportive community through family, friends, and church, this may end up being an incredible experience for all of you.

If you're a single parent, are struggling to get by financially, or have some other circumstance that makes public school your best option, don't sweat it! The Lord knows your heart, and I encourage you to trust him in this season. Genuine conversations with your children about the influences in their schools and your hope that they will walk with Jesus every day will have more of an impact than you could imagine. God will provide one step at a time, and sending your kids to school may be his greatest provision for you in the season you're in.

No matter what educational route you choose, including homeschooling, it's wise to check in with your kids often. See how it's going. Ask questions. Listen. Be willing to consider making changes or trying something new. God will guide you as you prayerfully commit to training your child in the way they will go. Trust him to lead!

Sports

Sports have played a huge role in raising my boys, and I know they're a staple for families across the world. I want to spend a little time speaking about the important role they can play in our children's lives. Participation in sports is one of my favorite ways to offer children a healthy, non-screen activity as well as social experiences, character-building opportunities, and many life lessons.

Recently I asked a series of questions on my Instagram story related to people's experience raising kids in youth sports: What do you love about youth sports? What is your greatest challenge related to youth sports? and more. The responses confirmed some of our own experiences and opened my eyes to others.

From the cost of youth sports (much too high, some said) to the commitment level (too much at a young age, others said), some definite negatives were expressed. But other people credit sports with much of their children's personal growth and development. Their family gladly plans their calendar around their kids' sports and hopes to keep it going to the college level.

For Dave and me, sports have always been a huge part of our lives. We both grew up playing traditional team sports as well as individual sports. Some of our first dates consisted of mountain bike rides and gym workouts, and we still run together often.

When we had kids, we naturally signed up our boys for the sports we loved. But after a few years of trying to convince them they might learn to love soccer, we had to accept that it wasn't their passion. We also tried basketball and martial arts. The boys finally found their happy place between the local skatepark and on a surfboard at the beach. *All new territory for us.*

Though we've continued to give our boys team-sports experiences as we can, considering our homeschool life in Hawaii, most of them have settled on individual pursuits. As I've mentioned, all our boys love to surf, and our third son, Luke, is currently surfing professionally. More recently, as I mentioned earlier, our youngest has decided that golf is his passion, so we're now learning about wedges and woods, bunkers and bogies. It isn't cheap, so that's a constant conversation. But I'm learning as I go, and I love that Dave is all-in, learning about golf alongside Levi.

Suffice it to say, there's a lot we could talk about when it comes to youth sports.

Our kids will each have their unique experiences, but I hope you'll consider the benefits of sports for your children. Sports will impact their life well beyond the gymnasium or field—their bodies, minds, and character will be shaped.

Here are two of those benefits.

1. It's Healthy to Play Sports!

With obesity, diabetes, and heart disease on the rise with our screen-addicted youth culture, it's hard to argue with all the health benefits of sports. Though some sports are more active than others (after all, chess is officially a sport!), almost all sports will provide some physical benefits. Sports offer kids activity, fresh air, muscle building, flexibility, and much more. Your kids may decide sports are not for them when they're grown, but it's in their best interest to give them a healthy foundation. Sports are a great way to do that.

Even more, research has shown that teenagers who participate in physically active team or individual sports are less likely than sedentary kids to drink, smoke, use drugs, have sex, or take other health risks. Physically active students are also likely to have higher self-esteem and better grades. That's a good motivation to begin with.[2]

Kids with disabilities benefit as well. The American Association of Pediatrics did a study that showed kids with disabilities benefit from participation in physical activity in numerous ways. While doctors and caregivers often focus on the risks involved in sports, children with disabilities who participate in adaptive or therapeutic sports or recreation have shown improved mental health, improved physical functioning, higher academic achievement, and enhanced overall well-being.[3]

If you've ever experienced an elevated mood after a good run or bike ride, I'm sure you won't doubt the overall health benefits for a growing child to get exercise. It's just plain good for you!

2. Sports Promote Character Development

I can't think of a more powerful, effective way to build character in our kids than to involve them in sports. My friend Carla, who's raising football and soccer players in Texas, joined me for a sports chat on my podcast, and I love what she said about sports and character: "Competitive sports are the best place for kids to learn to win with humility and lose with integrity."

The character qualities we so desperately want to teach our kids at home can be learned in real time by training, submitting to a coach, getting along with teammates, facing fears, overcoming adversity, winning or losing, and persevering through difficult seasons.

Here are a few of the many character qualities gained through sports.

A HARD-WORK ETHIC

Clearly, to be excellent at anything requires hard work. Sports give kids a chance to experience discipline and sweat. We often remind our boys of the biblical call to put their whole heart into whatever they do, referencing Colossians 3:23: "Whatever you do, work at it with all your heart, as working for the Lord, not for human masters."

THE ABILITY TO FOLLOW RULES AND SUBMIT TO AUTHORITY

Kids need to learn to submit to authority and follow rules. This will be key to their education, future jobs, service in the military, or in any other area of life. By learning to listen to a coach and accept the call of a judge, referee, or umpire, your kids will learn self-control and restraint. At some point your child will disagree with those who make the calls, and that prepares them for real life, which often isn't fair.

A WILLINGNESS TO COMPETE IN A HEALTHY WAY

In Luke's surfing career, we've often reminded him that his buddies are "friends on land, competitors in the water!" Competition is part of life, but handling it well isn't always easy. Sports can help with this, especially if a coach or parent trains kids to do it well.

AN UNDERSTANDING OF TEAMWORK

Involved in team sports, kids learn to work for something bigger than themselves—a team is depending on them. How they act or play will affect their teammates. Even showing up for practice is important when you're on a team. Teamwork skills will benefit a child in future jobs as well as in their family life.

PATIENCE

Having to wait your turn in practice, sit on a bench during a game (or an entire season), and practice for weeks before games or tournaments begin requires great patience. Anything good is worth waiting (and working) for.

KNOWING HOW TO LOSE WELL

Losing is part of the human experience. Let's make sure our kids know how to lose with dignity and good character. An unknown author said, "How you play shows some of your character, how you win or lose shows all of it."

ACQUIRED GRIT

Many people criticize the younger generations because they tend to give up when things are hard. Parents may be to blame for making life too easy for their kids; many say we've protected and coddled them. Regardless of who's to blame, be assured that sports will help with that—especially if we step back, let our kids face hard times, and don't let them quit when participation becomes a challenge.

In fact, if you have the tendency to helicopter or snowplow in your parenting, putting your kids on a team and getting out of the way may be the best thing for all of you!

Note: Find a list of fifteen character-inspiring quotes from great athletes in the resource section.

If you have the tendency to helicopter or snowplow in your parenting, putting your kids on a team and getting out of the way may be the best thing for all of you!

3. Be Aware of the Potential Downside to Youth Sports

Certain sports are time-consuming, so count the cost before getting involved. If a sport requires more than you're willing to give, you might look for a recreational version or completely steer clear of it.

Sports can also cost a small fortune. Some sports are expensive! Especially if you have several kids involved in sports, it sometimes doesn't pencil out as financially reasonable to sign them all up. If your child is passionate about a sport, though, you might investigate scholarships or local funds that can help.

Specialization has gotten *cray-zee*. Most of the kids who end up going pro or competing in the Olympics probably start off very young. This might rub you wrong. Some kids struggle with team sports, and the frustration drags them down more than builds them up. If this is the case, you might consider individual sports or healthy activities the family can do together (hiking, swimming, tennis, and so on).

Personally, I love to dream big. If my kids want to go pro, I'll cheer them on until we know whether it's remotely possible. This topic will be personal to your family, so talk about it as early as you can.

I should also mention that a coach makes all the difference. If you grew up doing sports, you probably remember a few good coaches and at least one terrible one. If you have some options on coaches for the sport your child is interested in, take some time to ask questions and do your research. But much of the time we don't get to choose. If that's the case, keep conversations open with your child about what's going on at practices and during games. In extreme cases, you might need to confront a coach or pull your child from a team, but much of the time your child will just learn and grow from even tough situations.

All the Extracurriculars

Although I love youth sports for many reasons, and I believe all kids should have an active lifestyle, I do want to mention that there are a whole lot of extracurriculars that might also shape our kids and prepare them for an amazing future. In our family, the boys have all taken music lessons at some point, and so far three of them have been willing to keep playing an instrument. (I won't name names, but perhaps by this point you can guess which [youngest] child doesn't want to practice his music!)

We often choose our kids' activities based on what's convenient and what our friends are doing. That's a good start. But I also encourage you to consider what your child is drawn to. Is your toddler obsessed with balls? Maybe your little girl twirls and whirls throughout her days. Does your child love gardening or painting? Maybe your child sings all day long or loves fiddling with mechanical things. These are all things to note and consider.

My best advice is to let your kids try a lot of different things. Depending on where you live and what's available and cost, introduce them to one thing at a time. If something sticks, good. If they don't love something, let it go.

As for our family, we love art and have tried to keep art supplies on hand and find art classes for kids to plug into. My oldest son is passionate about photography, and all my boys have learned to edit videos and be creative online. Also, following in their dad's footsteps, each of my sons have grown to be true bird nerds. (Oops. I mean very cool birding people.)

I could go on and on about all the interesting ways my boys have spent their free time—from building simple furniture to harvesting fruit and selling it on the street in front of our house, from catching fish and finding the best recipes to prepare it, to claymation and writing poems and stories. As I mentioned before, Jonah hosted his own podcast during his gap year between high school and college (look for *The Truth for Youth Podcast* link in the resource section), and Josiah published an adventure book titled *Sub-Marine* when he was eighteen based on stories he developed with his brothers growing up. A lot of parents have enjoyed reading this with their kids, and I'll also put a link to it in the resource section.

The following questions might be helpful to consider as you guide your kids to choosing activities:

- *What is my motivation for signing up for this? Is my child interested? Or is this more about my interests?* To be fair, sometimes kids have no idea what they like until they try it. But sometimes we place our interests on our kids and try to force things. This may take some discernment (and honesty), but make sure you aren't living out your own childhood through your kids.
- *Is it good for my child in the age and stage they're in? Will it be good for us as parents?* Sometimes the idea is good, but the timing is not. Use wisdom as you navigate.
- *If my child enjoys this activity, am I willing to stick with it?* I was excited to sign Jonah up for Speech and Debate club, but then I realized he had to go to practices on the other side of the island, about an hour and a half's drive away from our home, and I also needed to be there with him for the long tournament days. I'm so glad we could work it out, but I did have some adjustments to make!
- *Will this activity get in the way of other priorities?* One year our boys took a martial arts class that was literally smack in the middle of dinner hour. We worked it out for a season, but it just wasn't realistic to change our lifestyle for the long-term. Some sports schedule games on Sunday mornings, when you want to be in church, or Saturday mornings, when your family might savor a slow start to the day. Consider all the ways an activity might interfere with, or adjust, your family's priorities before signing up.

Each of our kids will grow up with a unique memory bank, full of the everyday moments, the highlights and the hardships of life. We can't write their stories for them, but we certainly can provide opportunities and coach them through these special years of youth. Prayerfully consider the treasure of childhood as you invest time into your kids' days. How fun it will be to sit around the table years down the road and recount all the moments that made up the memories they carry with them.

A Word to Dads

Dads, your kids' education will be a huge part of their life. I encourage you to be a part of this conversation and the related decisions. Do a bit of research on the direction public schools are going and anything else you can find on the educational options in your community.

I was hesitant when Monica brought up homeschooling; I had the "homeschooled kids are weird" belief going into it. But now I'm so glad we gave it a try. And maybe my kids are a little weird—but in a good way! I've loved the time homeschooling has given me with my kids and the way I believe it's shaped their character and helped lead to the success they're having now.

Whatever you choose to do for your kids' schooling, commit to being involved in their education and in their lives throughout the years. I read a quote by George Herbert that says, "One father is more than a hundred schoolmasters." Realize that your kids are taking in the things you say a lot more than you know. So be intentional, be involved, and be prayerful about your kids and their education.

As for sports and extracurriculars, this is the fun stuff! Inside each of your kids are gifts and talents— some good genes from each of their parents, you can hope. You get the job of discovering what they are and how to bring them out.

Life can be busy while you're raising kids, but don't

forget to play too. You probably remember how much it meant to you when your dad tossed a ball with you or took you fishing. Remember that, and then make plans with your own kids. Try not to look at everything like a task or something they have to be good at. Just enjoy them.

Because I loved soccer so much, it was honestly hard for me when my boys weren't that into it. (Some of them mostly hated it.) But as I let go of my agenda for them, I learned to enjoy what they loved. I learned alongside them. And I tried to do the things they did. (I dropped into a skate bowl for the first time at forty.)

If you've got daughters, think of all the things you might do with them to make them feel loved and cherished. Play with them. Watch them and listen to them. Learn about the activities they love and support them the best you can. They say if you listen to your kids' silly stories when they're young, they'll trust you to listen to the more serious stuff when they're teenagers. That's what you want: a relationship with them as they grow up!

Because guys aren't always good at the eye-to-eye talks, sports and hobbies present a good opening for us to communicate with our kids. While you're hiking or biking or building or doing art, you can bring up things that might be less comfortable to talk about while sitting across a table.

Help your children figure out what they love, and then cheer them on to do it well. They'll need lots of encouragement and support. Make sure they know your love isn't based on their performance. Keep perspective (it's easy to get competitive) and trust that they'll eventually find their passions and interest. Guard yourself against trying to live out your dreams through your kids.

Remember, God has a plan unique to each of your kids, and he can use you to help develop it. Now go have fun. You've got this!

Thoughts from Jonah, Age Twenty

One of the great benefits of growing up as a homeschooler was the opportunity to explore many extracurricular activities outside of school and without much limitation. I didn't have to choose from a list of clubs or sports within one school. Instead, I had the freedom to explore extracurricular activities all over our area. These sports, clubs, and extracurricular involvements played a crucial role in shaping who I am today, and they continue to shape me now.

Some of my favorite activities during high school were participating in Speech and Debate club, playing guitar, surfing, running cross-country, being in book clubs, and sharing in ministry opportunities through my church. As I entered college, I continued my pursuit of extracurriculars and sports because of how important they were to my prior development and life. I joined the Young Life ministry organization as a leader, became involved in a worship club on campus, eventually joined the track team, and pursued many other activities as well.

It's important to realize the role extracurricular

activities and sports play in a kid's and a young adult's life and to find as much time to explore these activities as you can. The things you do for your own pleasure and enjoyment rather than out of obligation are most likely to stick with you in the end.

Reflection Questions

1. If you imagine your kids as young adults, which memories do you hope will stand out to them and you?

2. What do you hope your kids will get from their school experience? How are you planning their education so they're built up mentally, physically, and spiritually?

3. What interests or talents do your kids have that might point to an activity they could thrive in?

4. When you consider the years you have with your children, what do you think might be the best way to invest in the free time you currently have together?

CHAPTER 13

ALL THE SCREENS!

Make Good Choices about Technology

*It is absolutely, completely possible to make different
choices about technology from the default settings of
the world around us . . . It is possible to love and use
all kinds of technology but still make radical choices to
prevent technology from taking over our lives.*
—Andy Crouch

Every generation of parents faces unique challenges. Some parents raised kids in wartime or during a nation-wide financial crisis. Some raised kids during plagues or (ahem) pandemics. "Recreational" and illegal drugs have become more and more available during the last decades, and now we have a culture saturated in technology.

Yes, parents face plenty of challenges in each generation, but I'm convinced the rapid rise in the use of technology stands out as our greatest challenge as parents today.

For starters, technology is still so new. You may have had a smartphone in your hands since you were a teenager, but we don't have much in the way of research and statistics to help us navigate the digital saturation our kids are being raised in. (And let's face it, most grandmas are no help when we're looking for wisdom on a kid's TikTok use!)

With that, our kids are "digital natives" and seem to have been born with an innate understanding of technology. Updates and changes don't intimidate them. (It's really not fair.)

And what's more, technology is ever changing. The minute you think you "get" some part of it, like an app, something new comes out. Case in point, despite its current popularity, TikTok might have been replaced by the time you read this.

Yet none of those things gives us a pass as parents. We signed up for parenting, which means we signed up for screen navigation too. And we can rest assured that none of this is a surprise to God, the One who placed you and your kids in the world for such a time as this. God doesn't make mistakes; he knew you'd face this, and he will help you through it.

We signed up for parenting, which means we signed up for screen navigation too.

I've mentioned before that the environment I'm raising my youngest son in is a different world from that of his big brothers. Technology became central to lives and homes around the time my oldest boys were in middle school. By then, their core identities and personalities had been shaped by nature and books, Bible stories, Hot Wheels, and Legos. I mean, we had a TV, and they watched their fair share of cartoons and kids' movies on DVD, but our world had not yet been inundated with technology the way it is now.

Six and a half years after my third son was born, our youngest was born into a screen-obsessed, social-media-saturated world.

Over his twelve years of life, we've battled more over devices and screen time than anything else. Interestingly, he's hardly watched television ("TV is so last century"). But both big and small screens are all around him—in pockets and on desks, on Mom and Dad's phones, on a laptop here and an iPad there, all with a magnetic pull that's hard to comprehend or compete with.

We set boundaries the best we can, really. But the biggest problem might be the bad example set when the rest of us are on screens so much ourselves.

The struggle is real.

I'm determined not to give up on this battle. It matters. In fact, the more I research this topic of kids and screens, the more I grow convinced that, though our culture has normalized a screen-centric existence, we may look back one day with a very different perspective.

Care for a Smoke?

Smoking cigarettes used to be normal and common. For decades it was a socially acceptable habit that most people didn't judge or condemn, both in real life and in movies. It was all good and fine. Print ads even showed doctors and pregnant women smoking. Really! All of that went on until the medical community began to connect the dots between smoking and lung cancer, heart disease, and other deadly health issues.

Screens may not kill our kids the same way cigarettes can, but in a million other ways, they just might.

Parents, we don't have to give in to peer pressure or the idea that *this is just the way it is* when it comes to technology. We can manage differently! I'm not talking about living like the Amish or ignoring progress; I'm talking about intentionally setting firm boundaries, establishing rhythms, and helping our kids develop a healthy relationship with technology. Even when it's hard to do.

Establishing a Healthy Relationship with Technology

When we're navigating something challenging, I find it helpful to consider how we handle a different area of life we're more objective about. So since kids and technology can seem extra complex and overwhelming to many of us, I'd like to step away from the topic and consider how we might parent through something similar, even if it's not a perfect parallel. For example, we can consider kids and eating habits. Not that food is a simple part of parenting, but there's a good chance this isn't causing as much angst among parents as technology is.

Let's give this a shot.

Our kids need to eat every day, and it's up to us to first feed them a healthy diet, then teach them how to choose good foods for themselves. Most experts don't suggest completely restricting any entire category of food, which can backfire, but to focus on a nutritious diet, offering sweet treats or junk food as "sometimes" foods. We would never allow our kids to eat Oreos for breakfast, lunch, and dinner (though at least one of my sons would surely appreciate that). Instead, we ought to set boundaries and limit the unhealthy food in our homes—or at least hide it well! (Shh.)

Obviously, we don't let our toddler make the weekly meal plan, and we don't allow our twelve-year-old to crack open a beer with dinner. We are the parents. We make the rules. Of course, as our kids grow up, we can transfer more responsibility to them in hopes that they might make good decisions for themselves. But we don't release it all at once; we give them more autonomy as they prove responsible.

Kids aren't likely to appreciate the food boundaries you set, so don't expect them to. This isn't usually a fun part of parenting, but we know enough about health and nutrition to know it's worth it for us to stick to our guns. So we keep trying.

Now, the same basic approach can be applied to kids and screens. Yes, screens are here to stay, but that doesn't mean we should throw up our hands and allow our kids a free-for-all akin to a diet of strictly Oreos. We also don't restrict screen use completely. Instead, we're wise to set technology boundaries in the early years and talk to our kids about healthy and unhealthy choices.

Educational games or art apps are mostly healthy, but video games ought to be like junk food—a "sometimes" treat. And we want to completely block some sources to protect our kids from predators, pornography, and other dangers. For other things, we simply need to monitor and keep track of them, like how much time kids are on devices and what they're doing with that time. I find that when I'm unemotional and level-headed, I can make more reasonable choices with confidence.

> *Screens are here to stay, but that doesn't mean we should throw up our hands and allow our kids a free-for-all.*

Zoom Out on Your Child's Day

Before we get to specific guidelines, I think it helps to zoom out on a child's day as a whole.

We should be sure they're getting plenty of play. In the early years, offer an abundance of unstructured, imagination-led play. Add to that school, chores, sports (or some form of exercise), then consider what time is left. Has your child read or been read to today? How about music and art? Having a musical instrument and simple art supplies in an easy-to-reach spot will make it a lot more likely that kids will pick them up. If we've filled our kids' day with brain-stimulating creative outlets, there is unlikely to be a lot of time left to spend on screens.

What I'm saying is this: instead of allowing screens to *be the day*, what if you decided screens can land in the *what's left of the day* category? As a parent, you can make this choice! You can shift the focus of your home. It may take some time for the family to adjust—especially if you're in the habit of making screens the front and center of your day—but in time you'll all adapt.

It's easy to focus on and get all stressed about rules for screens and all the rest, when maybe a simple emphasis on all the good that's healthy and freely allowed is a better approach.

In a season when our boys were spending too much time on a video game, Dave hid our game console and challenged them to read twice as much. After the initial pushback, we were pleasantly surprised to see them fall deeper in love with great books.

I think a child who's developed hobbies and passions beyond a screen won't mind getting off a device when it's time. If they've drained their energy running and playing or crafting and creating, the magnetic pull of screens seems to decrease.

A Few Helpful Guidelines

Start with a Contract

One of the simplest ways to avoid arguments and be objective is to sign technology contracts. When we walked our boys through a cell phone contract, I saw that it brought them a greater sense of responsibility. The phone wasn't just a toy. It was a mature tool, and with it came a chance to show us they could make good choices that might earn them future freedoms. By signing their name on a contract, our kids realized they were owning the responsibility to use the device as we outlined. They knew that if they broke the contract, they'd lose the phone. (Find a link to sample contracts in this book's resources section.)

Apply Filters

My biggest recommendation is always for families to apply filters on every device their child has access to. Of all dangers on the internet, pornography is my number one concern, and for good reason. Data from 2018 show that . . .

- "57% of teens search out porn at least monthly.
- 51% of male students and 32% of female students first viewed porn before their teenage years.
- The first exposure to pornography among men is 12 years old, on average.
- 71% of teens hide online behavior from their parents."[1]

These statistics and many others are a big reason to use filters. Many options for them and for accountability software exists, and these companies can send you reports anywhere from daily to weekly. (Also, find some suggested filters in my resources section at the back of this book.)

It is important to note, however, that filters are not foolproof. Typical filtering software does not work within an app (like YouTube, Google Earth, etc.). It will take time and energy to become familiar with any technology our kids use and to set filters within apps (which you can do!). And even if we do everything we know of to protect our kids, they still may view pornography on a friend's device or by sneaking around filters. (Where there is a will there is a way.) This is why I always say that a healthy relationship with regular conversations is your first defense against online dangers.

Don't Allow Screens in Bedrooms

Jonathan McKee, author of *Parenting Generation Screen*, says that "hands down, no screens in bedrooms" is his number one recommendation! He goes on to say, "This isn't an oversimplification.

It's just that after thirty years of working with young people, raising three kids of my own, working in social research, and hearing parents share countless problems and frustrations with their kids, I've learned that screens in the bedroom are a common denominator for trouble."[2]

One of the many reasons screens in bedrooms are a bad idea is the tendency for teens with screens to sleep less. And less sleep leads to a lot of other negative things, like academic challenges and depression. McKee cited a study showing that for each hour of lost sleep, the odds of teens feeling sad or hopeless increased by 38 percent, and the risk of attempted suicide increased by 58 percent.[3] That is crazy! I am paying attention.

Fortunately, there's an easy way to help kids get more sleep: get screens out of their rooms! Have a "charging station" in the parents' bedroom or in the living room. Then be sure to implement this rule on the daily!

Require Parental Approval for All Apps

Set up all devices so that when your child tries to download a new app, the device sends you a notification and opportunity to "approve" (or not). This can be done through account settings on devices or through the app store. Take the time to set it up right away and save yourself the trouble later. If you learn your kids found a sneaky way to get an app without your approval, take the device away until they can earn your trust again. (This consequence can be included in the contract.)

Set Time Limits

We all want to know the magic numbers!

> "What's the right age to give a child their own phone/tablet/ laptop?"

"How much time is OK for a child to use a screen device?"
"At what age is it OK to allow a child to use social media?"
"How much time should kids get to play video games on
    weekdays, weekends, and so on?"

These are all good questions, and I only wish I had one good answer for each of them—for you and me both! But as with much good parenting, the answers will be unique to each child (or at least to each family) and will be based on many factors. We might begin with these guidelines from the American Academy of Child & Adolescent Psychiatry:

- "Until 18 months of age limit screen use to video chatting along with an adult (for example, with a parent who is out of town).
- Between 18 and 24 months screen time should be limited to watching educational programming with a caregiver.
- For children 2–5, limit non-educational screen time to about 1 hour per weekday and 3 hours on the weekend days.
- For ages 6 and older, encourage healthy habits and limit activities that include screens."[4]

Obviously, once children are six years old, the waters get muddy. Kids use screens for many things, and it's up to us to shape how that will look. If you want to customize a plan for your own family, you might want to check out the American Academy of Pediatrics website, which offers a Family Media Plan you can customize to your family's circumstances and goals.[5]

Set Regular Routines and Rhythms

If kids know that certain days or times are designated for screen time, that will relieve much of the stress for you and confusion for them. When I interviewed Justin Whitmel Earley on my podcast, he suggested using regular rhythms for the use of all our screen activities. I was busted when he talked about how it's just plain mean to parent with a *screen time might be anytime* mentality.

I realized then that I'd been doing exactly that with Levi. In my attempt to limit his screen use, I required him to ask permission to use our family iPad or computer, which put him in a constant state of *maybe*. Sometimes I'd say yes and let him play longer than I meant to; other times it was a quick no. There was no rhyme or reason other than how busy I was or the mood I was in. Since my chat with Justin, I settled on giving Levi forty-five minutes a day on our family iPad or computer when he can watch golf videos or play a game—*after* school, chores, and being active.

I'm far from perfect at implementing this new rule, but that one change has relieved a lot of stress.

More Practical Approaches to Screen Time

- Set a daily time limit for screens outside of schoolwork. Thirty minutes to an hour is reasonable for most kids, but you can decide.
- Have a system for kids to earn screen time and track it in a common area of the home. This might be thirty minutes for every thirty minutes of reading or exercise. Or it may be one hour when schoolwork and chores are complete. Track the plan on a whiteboard, and breaking these boundaries ought to have consequences.
- Set a specific day that's officially movie night or video game night.

Good parenting is hard. We can do hard things.

Phones and Tablets

Choosing when to give your child their own device will depend on your family circumstances as well as how responsible your kids are, and how responsible you're willing to be to check in on what they're doing with that device, set controls, and so on. Bill Gates didn't even give his kids a cell phone until they were fourteen, so that's something to consider.[6]

With each of our kids, we've held off on giving them their own devices a little longer. We homeschool, they've usually had access to their father's or my screens when needed. Luke used a flip phone until he was nearly seventeen, and at some point he shifted from complaining to embracing it as *cool!* It was inconvenient in many ways, but again, he could use his parents' phones for posting videos on social media.

For all screen-related decisions in our family, we've chosen not to go by an age or grade level but by our sons' need for one, as well as their maturity and current ability to follow directions and honor their parents. As their level of responsibility increased, so did our trust, and we loosened the reins accordingly. Once again, this is one of the great challenges of parenting today, but it is not beyond our abilities.

Video Games

Most kids love video games, and many experts say plenty of positive benefits result when they're used well. Kids can learn teamwork, develop hand-eye coordination, problem-solving skills, improved self-worth, and even social skills from video games. I have argued that you could get all the same benefits and more by playing basketball or tennis, but I won't claim to be an expert on this one. I can accept that video games, used in moderation, are probably just fine.

Not all video games are created equal, however. I recommend checking the ratings and doing your due diligence to find out if the games your kids want to play contain violence, sexual content, and so on. Also, avoid allowing your younger kids to play games where strangers can meet them.

I interviewed a well-researched video gaming mom on my podcast (you read that right—a mom who loves video games!), and she offered a most-helpful list of guidelines for parenting young gamers. I'm sharing a link to them in my resources section at the end of this book.

Social Media

Social media is a big, complicated topic for any human being. Bringing still-developing kids into the conversation makes it even more complex. Social media brings together a potentially toxic combination of peer communication, images, video content, the internet, beauty filters, and 24/7 access to all of it. Oh, my. Wow. Where do we begin?

I don't think I need to tell you social media has potential danger for our teens. But research is proving that social media is especially concerning to girls.

An article on WebMD highlights research done at Imperial College London. The study showed that social media especially influenced girls' mental health in three main ways: "experiencing cyberbullying, sleeping for less than eight hours a night, and reduced physical activity." Girls were found to use social media more than boys, and "the more often they used social media, the more psychological distress they suffered." In addition, a well-being survey found that "girls who used social media very often were likely to report lower life satisfaction and happiness, and greater anxiety."[7]

Personally, I can't imagine how poorly I would have handled social media as a teenager! But though this study revealed social media has less of an impact on boys, I'm convinced that social media affects them in similar ways that it affects girls.

Parenting kids in a time like this can be extremely challenging. We want to protect them, but we also know social media is a part of the fabric of life in the world they're growing up in. It's a common way people communicate, and plenty of positive influences and inspirations are available on social media platforms.

The key, it seems, is once again helping our kids grow up with healthy boundaries and a grounded perspective on their use of social media. Here are important questions you might ask your teen:

1. **Why do you want to use social media? What is your goal or motivation?** This might sound silly to a thirteen-year-old, but it might also reveal some things you need to address before saying yes. Do they want to use social media to communicate with friends, follow celebrities, or grow in popularity by posting pictures of themselves and their life?

2. **Do you think you're mature, wise, and strong enough to handle all that comes with social media?** Talk about what cyberbullying is, how it feels to see friends together if you weren't invited to join them, and the great potential to fall into the comparison trap. While some teens are likely to be in denial, I've heard of plenty who, after discussing their readiness, confess they don't feel ready. (Smart kids.) They choose to wait a while. And I hope their parents reward them for that!

I Highly Recommend . . .

LIMITS

Just as with all screen use, I recommend setting limits on social media use. This is fairly easy to do using a time-limits option available on devices. My sons all have set time limits, and I set up a password that must be entered to extend their daily time. This is easy, built-in accountability.

TRUE BREAKS

Besides daily or weekly time limits, there ought to be established times when kids turn off their devices and put them away. Here are a few times and places we try to abide by: during dinner, in bedrooms at night, during classes or meetings, and when guests are in our home or our family is spending intentional time together (holidays, family devotions, and so on).

SABBATH BREAKS

A day off social media a week is an excellent idea. If a whole day is too much, then starting with half a day might be wise. In addition, it's wise to plan regular (annual? quarterly?) extended breaks from social media.

Let's Be Honest

Social media was created to be addictive. "Likes" and "follows" trigger a dopamine release in our brains, very similar to what a drug can. It's a lot of responsibility to put on a young teenager.

My sons have each fluctuated between enjoying social media and, frankly, hating it. They've admitted it causes them to struggle with comparison (me too!), and they've nearly deleted their accounts. At one point my oldest son took a break from it and reached out to a few men he respected—mostly pastors and leaders—to get their opinions.

One pastor from Southern California encouraged him by saying, "I figure if the apostles were alive today, they'd be on social media. It's how people get messages out. I see it as an opportunity to be a light." This was a helpful perspective, because, really, it all comes down to our motivation, right?

Like everything else, I recommend talking to your kids, checking in with them often, and coaching them through it all. They should know that anything they post (or text or direct message and so on) will potentially be somewhere on the internet forever, so they must be careful and wise about what they share.

Whew! We did it. We just scratched the surface of kids and screens, but I do hope you feel a little less alone now. Full books on each of the bullet points I've shared are available, so I encourage you to explore further as you need to. I also have a mini-course called Raising Tech-Smart Kids on my website, which has a more extensive list of resources and guidelines you might find helpful.[8] While it can feel super overwhelming to raise a child in this screen-saturated time, you really do have everything you need to do it well. Keep common sense in mind, and do not fear!

A Word to Dads

Your parental job of providing and protecting is a full-time operation. It's probably always been hard, and I'm sure it always will be. But this relatively new world of technology has made the job a whole lot harder.

Technology and its reach into our lives is changing faster than the microchip in tablets like the one you bought six months ago. If your family is like 99 percent of families, you have a screen that's in some way accessible to a child—and if it isn't, it soon will be. So you must be prepared to deal with all that comes with it.

Don't tune out on this one, my friend. Your kids' minds are precious. From them flows everything that makes your children who they are. Their beliefs about themselves, the world around them, the center for creativity and learning—it's all packaged in that little noggin of theirs. And it's connected to a high speed optical and auditory input system, otherwise known as eyes and ears.

Then it's all going into this incredible information-collection system, a data processing and decision-making center. Your child's mind is mission control. And here's the thing: your kid's mind is beautiful and amazing, fearfully and wonderfully made in every way. But it's highly vulnerable and needs protection. *Your protection.* Our kids' supercomputer minds have viruses and security threats coming at them constantly, and this expanding world of screens has upped the ante.

Our oldest son is studying data analytics, and what he's taught me helps me appreciate the power of marketing. Companies spend millions of dollars to make many more millions of dollars off us as consumers. A primary way they do this is by going after our kids. They know how to take advantage of the right words and images to capture a child's fragile mind. Messages that make them feel what they have isn't enough, how they look isn't good enough, or they need to be something more or have something more.

Over time, the social media giants lead our kids away from the security of a self-worth that's founded on God's truth about our infinite value in his eyes. It can cause them to devalue the unique qualities he's blessed them with. It then replaces God-given security and value with depression and despair. They're ultimately unable to live up to the unrealistic expectations of beauty or success. Or if they haven't given up, they're in a constant state of anxiety, expending energy on trying to maintain online relationships and gain "likes" or "follows" from people they don't even know.

I hate to paint such a dire picture, but this is reality, and as dads we need to help our kids through this.

Dads, we must talk to our children about pornography and other ways the Enemy perverts God's original and good plan for sex. Pornography has a power to addict young minds, and you need to rise up as protector and gatekeeper of your home. If you're not being proactive in this area, then your kids may already be losing this battle. Make sure to use a filter to regulate any device your kids have access to. Make sure they understand the responsibility of using the internet. Most of all, keep this conversation open. It's a big part of parenting in today's world.

I wish there were easy answers or a perfect step-by-step plan to parent well in this area of screens. I certainly haven't figured it all out myself. Technology keeps throwing curve balls. But one thing I know is that how I handle my own screens is setting a big example to my children. Sometimes the hardest part of parenting is modeling in this area, including how much time we spend on screens ourselves. But I'm convinced that raising amazing kids requires me to do these daily hard things, so I'll keep trying.

Thoughts from Luke, Age Eighteen

While traveling to train for surfing recently, I stayed with friends in San Clemente, California. They have kids who are a few years older than my brothers and I, and I love talking to them when we get together. During this visit, we got onto the topic of childhood one afternoon, and they asked me about my memories from growing up and being homeschooled in Hawaii.

I found myself excited to talk about it, because I really did have the best childhood. They asked me specifically about what stood out to be formative. Instantly, my mind rushed through scattered memories of my brothers and me in our childhood yard, running and playing. I recalled the outrageous yet amazing stories we made up, based on our imaginations, pretending we were inside them.

I thought of all the time spent at the beach, going for hikes with our parents, and playing sports. I remembered all the times we were in the car begging to hear the next audio chapter of our favorite series, Adventures in Odyssey, while we drove around the island.

As I rattled on about my childhood memories, it occurred to me that the most foundational components of my childhood all involved my imagination and pure, simple play.

None of them involved screens.

Now, I admit, I spend a lot of time on devices, mostly editing surfing videos, communicating with sponsors, and studying surfboarding, which I believe are good things. But I also communicate a *lot* with friends, spend a *lot* of time on social media, and watch a *lot* of entertainment.

Because of my lifestyle, my twelve-year-old brother has adopted similar habits as much as he's allowed.

Before I continue, I have to point out that technology is a big part of how our culture functions now, and a lot of good can come from it. Together, my little brother and I find a lot of funny, informative, and inspiring things online, and sometimes we even find things that inspire us to do something cool ourselves. Yet it goes without saying that bad can come out of the internet, too, and that more often than not it does.

To keep it short, I think this recent conversation with our friends in California made me want to put more limits on my screen time and encourage my parents to keep putting limits on my little brother's screen time. I've recognized that a huge part of growing up and developing and maturing comes from our own self-developed imagination, and I don't want my little brother or me to miss out on the great, screen-free adventures right in front of us.

I understand it's no easy task, but I think small steps are good, and we'll all look back and be thankful for the amazing times we made possible with our own God-given imagination.

Reflection Questions

1. How would I describe each of my family members' current "relationship" with technology and screens?

2. What is an area where I might set new guidelines or limits for the health and safety of my children?

3. How would I describe my own relationship with technology (social media, screens in general), and which changes might I need to make to be a better example to and leader for my family?

CHAPTER 14

FIRST TRACKS

Talk to Your Kids about Everything

*The most influential of all educational factors is
the conversation in a child's home.*
—William Temple

Our family went on a snowboarding trip to Oregon last Christmas, and we traveled during the Pacific Northwest's first serious snowstorm of the season. The first morning we arrived at the slopes was a sight to behold: several feet of fresh snow had fallen, and it looked like a winter wonderland. As we made our way to the top of the lift, my husband looked out over the hill with a satisfied smile. "OK, family. We get to make some of the first tracks on this slope!" This was a moment none of us will ever forget.

My friend and author Kari Kampakis wrote a blog post about how we as parents should "set the first tracks" in parenting. She compared the ski slope to our child's mind.

As parents, we instinctively protect their mind. We keep our kids in safe environments and guard their innocence to the best of our ability. And though this is a great instinct, we must remember that our kids will be exposed to things sooner than we tend to believe. In mere seconds, their pristine view of the world can be interrupted by a peer, a Google search, or some random event that leaves a negative mark.[1]

With this in mind, we must have the potentially uncomfortable yet important conversations with our kids, preemptively. Kari went on to say, "As parents, we want to set the first tracks. We want to ski down first and impress the truth in our kids' minds so that when other skiers come behind us, our kids know which tracks to trust."[2]

Parents, it's not only part of our job but a high calling on our part to set the first tracks for our kids. I'm a big believer in talking to our kids about . . . well, just about everything! As we raise kids in a culture that's antagonistic toward biblical values, this is more necessary every year. We don't want to assume our kids know or understand how to apply the values we've taught them to specific issues that come up, so we must speak to them openly, honestly, *and often*.

Talk to Your Kids about Everything

"Talk about things before they are things." This was advice a friend gave me years ago, and it's proven to be incredibly helpful. Of course, we need to use good judgment and discernment. I'm not suggesting you discuss the hazards of STDs with your toddler or diagram the effects of drugs on the brain for your first grader (though that's not too far off). But I am suggesting you be prayerful and thoughtful, that you keep your parental antennas out, taking note of what you see in the neighborhood and in the news.

Does your child seem curious about body parts? Or ask a

question about race or politics that shows they're trying to make sense of the world around them? These are all helpful indicators, and they should spur us on to open important conversations before somebody else (or the internet) does.

Whose Opinion Matters?

My goal is not for my kids to embrace their parents' opinions; we're imperfect people who are likely to make mistakes and judgment errors. Instead, I want them to know and follow God's truths. He is the source of all truth, and his standards never change. Therefore, it's crucial that we teach our kids to always look at the world through the lens of the Bible. We should turn to God's Word as we discuss important topics with our children, and we should study God's Word for ourselves. The more I know the heart and character of God, the more I'll be ready to give a biblical response to issues that arise.

In time, our kids will have the freedom to form their own views and opinions, but as we open healthy dialogue, pointing them to the truth from God's Word, we can pray that the biblical tracks we set are deep and enduring. I will touch on the main topics that come up the most during the tween and teen years, but the important idea here is that of offering our children a biblical worldview—a lens through which to see the world and all the issues they will face—that is based on the unchanging truth of biblical principles. Note: In the resource section, I share a list of my favorite books and curriculum to help give your kids a biblical worldview.

Identity

Any child growing up today will receive an abundance of messages about who they are and what defines them: Funny. Smart.

Athletic. Musical. Any skin tone from black to white, short or tall, thin or fat. They'll hear many voices telling them their value is connected to what they look like or what they do. People's opinions will vary from day to day. Our kids' popularity will fluctuate with their friends. "Likes" and "follows" on social media can boost their ego or burst their bubble. Kids can go from hero to zero in the blink of an eye. But whether a label builds them up or tears them down, it will never offer the lasting security our kids were made for.

Instead, we want to point our children to the truth of who they are in Christ. The unchanging nature of being a child of God. He's the same yesterday, today, and tomorrow. Only God can make that promise. And only a child who puts their stake in that ground will be unshakeable.

The first three chapters of Ephesians is a great place to learn more about the identity we have as Christ followers. There, we see that, as God's children, we are *chosen, adopted, accepted, redeemed, forgiven, and loved.* Wouldn't having those concepts crystalized in a child's mind help them when anxiety, rejection, loneliness, fear, shame, or confusion come knocking? Instead of those taking up residence in their hearts, another voice will be calling out within them, saying, *You're God's chosen, safe, and forgiven child!*

When a child experiences disappointment or rejection (or a viral video of them slipping in the school cafeteria in horrifying embarrassment), they can trust in the fact that their true, core identity is rock solid. Not based on what they do, but based on who God is and what he says about them.

Dave and I both began to understand our identity in Christ in our early adult years, so it was still fresh on our minds when we had kids. We certainly haven't done everything right in parenting, but one thing we have tried to do right is intentionally talk to our sons about their identity in Christ from a young age . . . and keep the conversation going. We knew the world would offer them all kinds of messages and labels.

Then social media entered our world during our first son's early teenage years and added more confusion to the equation. We knew we couldn't protect our boys from every worldly message, but we hoped to offer them so much good truth that it would give them a line of defense against the lies of the world.

In the years since high school, our older boys have reflected on times in their teenage years when they felt like they didn't fit in and struggled with comparison or confidence. I'm happy to hear that in the quiet moments when they wrestled with their identity or self-worth, the truths we'd taught them from Scripture came back to them. Those didn't take away the struggles but did strengthen them in the midst of them.

We must tell our kids the truth about who they are and whose they are before the world feeds them lies.

> *We must tell our kids the truth about who they are and whose they are before the world feeds them lies.*

Gender and Sexuality

When I was a kid, I remember meeting someone new and immediately asking how old they were. And maybe what sport they played. (I was a tomboy.) Last week, over postchurch pancakes, Levi's friends told us that at their middle school, kids greet someone new by first asking, "What are you?" (as in, "What is your sexual orientation or gender pronoun?") I won't go into all the concerns I have on this topic, but we can agree that gender and sexuality topics are, without a doubt, a sign of our times.

I'm so thankful to have the authority of the Bible to give us an unchanging understanding of God's view of gender and sexuality.

Though our world makes it complicated, it doesn't have to be. We can begin conversations with our kids at a young age, by looking at Genesis, where we're told God created man and woman. Marriage, between one man and one woman for a lifetime, was God's idea. *Sex* was God's idea! A blessing—useful for procreation and to bond a man and woman in a unique and special way in marriages that represent the relationship between Christ and the church.

If you don't set "first tracks" about sexuality based on the biblical view at home, your child is more likely to accept the unbiblical view a whole world out there is ready to give them. The current cultural message is to fill every appetite, satisfy every craving, indulge every desire. "You do you" and "Love is love" reverberate through streets and school hallways and across all forms of media. But that is not based on truth, and it will never satisfy our God-given design. Godly character restrains human impulses and submits to a higher standard of behavior. Those who have been redeemed by God's love view their self-denial as an investment in their eternal rewards. Hardships and sacrifices are "light and momentary" in comparison to the eternal glory that far outweighs them all!

Standing on a biblical view of gender and sexuality will be challenging in our current culture, but we must. At the same time, our kids need to know that God loves all people and that we should never be mean or hurtful to anyone. We are told to love our neighbors, not just those we agree with. However, loving people is not the same as affirming their choices. We don't have to affirm or embrace someone's lifestyle to show them God's love.

So indeed, we have a great responsibility as Christians to speak the truth in love and to teach our kids to do that as well. And while Hollywood and the media try to create and normalize ungodly definitions of sex and gender for our children to buy into, we can raise kids who courageously stand on what's true.

Some of your children have likely already been exposed to confusing messaging about gender and sexuality, and if so, your child may question God's Word, your family values, or their own sexual identity. Unfortunately, I hear from more and more parents who are facing this. I sense the fear and concern in every message, and I am so sorry. Depending on your child's age and their personal faith, the best way to respond will vary. But I want to encourage you to hold on to hope and to believe that God can give you everything you need to navigate through these issues.

This is a big topic—too big for this book and beyond my expertise—but helpful resources are available if you're facing this situation (see a list in the resource section). Your presence and loving guidance in your child's life can make all the difference in the world if they're wrestling with these things. I'm praying for you!

Pornography

Pornography is on the tip-top of my *talk about things before they are things* list. Sadly, it's not a matter of *if* but *when* your kids will stumble upon pornography. So do not wait to set the first tracks.

I'm a big fan of using the book *Good Pictures Bad Pictures: Porn-Proofing Today's Young Kids* to introduce children to the topic of pornography. The junior edition is great for early elementary school kids, and the original book is designed for eight–to twelve-year-olds. I think my oldest son was fifteen when I got the original book, and I still went through it with him.

However you decide to bring up the topic, just be sure you do! I'm generally not a big believer in using scare tactics on children, but I do use them when I talk about two things: drugs and pornography. And for good reason. These are both topics worthy of the right kind of fear.

Yes, there is grace for mistakes and our kids need to know that from the start. But let's make sure they're clear on the dangers and addictive nature of and potential damage from pornography. And let's be sure to do our job to protect devices and little eyes from accidentally stumbling upon it as well.

Relationships, Dating, and Marriage

Our kids' views on dating and marriage begin long before they enter that season of life. They pick up messages from their parents, other people, and the culture around them. For this reason, I encourage parents to begin talking openly about God's plan for marriage early. Lay the first tracks by intentionally bringing it up while kids are young.

We already discussed marriage in chapter 5, so I won't go too far into all the ways you can model a healthy marriage. But it should be a central theme in your family life. Whether or not you're married, I hope you can find healthy ways to talk about marriage, giving your kids anticipation and hope for their own marriages.

A lot of people ask me what our family's "rules" are about dating. I have to confess we've never had any! We talk plenty about making wise choices in all areas of growing up, but my sons will tell you we didn't focus on a list of rules for this one.

Thus far, all three of my older boys have chosen not to "date" in high school. They've had a lot of good friends and spent much of their social time in the context of our small-town youth group that became more like extended family than friends, but they were intentional about not dating.

The oldest was first, deciding that dating in high school was pointless. He planned to go away to college and couldn't see a good reason to get involved in a relationship before then. He's a logical kid, and I won't say this is a formula or pattern for everyone, but I respected his choice. (He was invited to a prom dance, but things like that were all on a friend basis.)

His younger brothers followed in his footsteps. I've wondered if any of them might have weakened in their resolve if just the right girl showed up, and it's possible, but it never happened. There's no doubt that living in a small town in the country, being homeschooled, and growing up with all-boy siblings were factors that supported their decision.

Once in college, my two older boys were eager to date. By dating, I mean they took girls to coffee, the beach for a walk or a surf, or out for dinner a few times. For the most part they've both approached dating from a conservative (OK, maybe even an old-fashioned) angle.

JP Pokluda's book *Outdated* released while the boys were in college and encouraged their natural position. In it, he said, "The world may have a lot of rules for dating. But the Bible, which many people (wrongly) think of as a big book full of rules, has very few dating rules." And he went on to say,

> Besides listing those relatively few clear sins to avoid, the Bible is full of wisdom principles we can use to find incredible life in dating. They are not so much rules to be followed as they are good ideas that will never steer us wrong. Really, most of these would be considered common sense, but unfortunately sense is not all that common anymore, especially when it comes to something as emotionally charged as dating.[3]

Since our boys grew up reading the book of Proverbs like taking a daily vitamin, this resonated with them. They all hope to get married and have lots of children, and they want to do it right. So they're approaching dating with intentionality and wisdom. They pray for their future wives and are purposeful about the young women they spend time with.

I loved the example Pokluda shared in the first chapter of *Outdated*. He tells the story of going shopping with a friend who was looking for a specific item. While his friend shopped with a critical eye, Pokluda wandered around needing nothing in particular but becoming interested in everything in general. He wrote, "Both my friend and I were technically doing the same thing— 'Shopping'—but our experiences could hardly have been more different. He was on a mission; he had an objective and a purpose. I, on the other hand, was just playing around, I was shopping for fun."[4]

I'm sure you recognize the parallel to how people might approach dating. The "just for fun" approach to dating can lead to what the world calls fun. But most of us who've done it would agree that it's often a whole lot of mess and heartbreak. Teaching our kids to be "on a mission" for a God-given partner for life is an entirely different experience. My boys like this idea.

I know some young people fall in love and live happily ever after. I'm a fan of young love, done right. I simply think we need to raise our kids to understand God's plan and purpose for marriage and to recognize that their dating experience—however they decide to approach it—will impact their story for better or for worse.

Culture, Politics, and So On

It seems the past decade has provided us with more than our fair share of opportunities to talk about cultural issues, politics, and how our values play out in the world today. While I have often wanted to ignore the news and wish away the conflict and upheaval around us, I realize these are all opportunities to help our kids both understand and articulate a biblical worldview as it applies to each topic.

When topics of race were all over the news in the summer of 2020, Dave and I realized we had not talked to our boys a lot about racial issues. Living in the multiethnic Hawaiian Islands, our kids' experience has been different from those in other areas, but we found great resources by godly men and women to learn from and share with our kids. This led to some important conversations about history, culture, and how we can be a part of healing and unity in the world we live in.

When the topic of abortion comes up on the news, we have the opportunity to talk to our kids about the sanctity of life and discuss how we as Christ followers should respond to the cultural debate. None of these issues are simple, but these conversations have been so good.

We set examples by voting in our elections and praying regularly for our elected officials. When someone is elected that we do not prefer, or decisions are made that we disagree with, we remind our kids (and ourselves) of the blessing of knowing that ultimately God is king, and he is sovereign to work all things together for good in his timing.

Whether or not you're passionate about politics, as Christians we should teach our kids to focus on biblical values as they make voting decisions or form opinions on laws or policies. Jesus followers face the same issues as the rest of society, but we approach politics differently because of our faith and eternal perspective.

Romans 13:1–7 is a helpful passage to teach our kids what God thinks about our government. The apostle Paul instructs Christians to submit to authorities, pay taxes, and honor their leaders (among other things). Even more, in 1 Timothy 2:1–2, he instructs that "petitions, prayers, intercession and thanksgiving be made for all people—for kings and all those in authority, that we may live peaceful and quiet lives in all godliness and holiness." (See also Jesus's words in Matthew 22:21.)

The Future

From the time our children are little, we naturally bring up all they have ahead. We ask them what they want to be when they grow up, and we encourage them to dream big dreams. I loved dreaming with my little boys about their future—from being a trash collector (what is it about boys and a love for garbage trucks?) to inventing a time machine, becoming a pastor, or becoming the next Tiger Woods. (I'll let you guess which dream was each of my sons'!)

But at some point during their growing-up years, I watched each of my three older boys transition from childish dreaming about their future to "Oh, shoot! I have to be a grown-up pretty soon!" Just yesterday Levi brought up his sudden realization that he will have to choose a job one day. (You know, if the pro golfing thing doesn't work out. "Though it probably will!" he assures me.) I recall long chats with each of my older sons when they mapped out different pathways they might take and how each one might or might not work out. As much as I want my kids to savor their childhood, I am glad to see them realizing the responsibilities that lie ahead.

In today's culture a lot of grown men continue to live like children. They are irresponsible and lack a work ethic. They quit school or a job when it gets difficult. Too many men are numbing out on video games, pornography, or substances.

It's not just the men either. Many young ladies are also lost in today's culture. They lack direction and lose interest in anything that takes a long time or requires patience. They choose attention and image over character and conviction. Many factors feed into this (hello, social media and Hollywood!), but as parents we must realize what a crucial role we can play in helping our kids raise the bar and live with purpose and intention.

So let's talk to our kids about their futures—in light of their interests and passions but also in light of the fact that the world will not go easy on them. Let's help them develop a vision that's exciting and fulfilling—*and reasonable*. Support their ambitions, but also talk about the cost of living. Dream about falling in love, but also talk about what it costs to love well.

We can and should have many wonderful conversations with our kids as they near the launch phase. Some should be about practical things (make sure they know how to scramble an egg, change a tire, and manage a bank account, to name a few). Some about social or moral things (men should still open doors for women, and no one should ever lie or cheat or ever, ever, ever take drugs, just for starters). And plenty about all the things that require wisdom (the book of Proverbs is helpful for that).

As a parent, you'll have your own list of things you believe are mildly or wildly important to pass on to your kids. Some of yours will be different from mine. But it's important for you to have these conversations with your kids over time, not on the drive to college or the week before they get married! Begin the conversations early. And keep having them. To help you get started, in the resource section, I have a list of important conversations to have before your kids launch. I hope it's just a springboard for you to come up with some of your own.

It's important for you to have these conversations with your kids over time, not on the drive to college or the week before they get married!

Talk about Amazing . . .

What a wonderful opportunity we have to bring up kids who are critical thinkers, know God's truth, and aren't afraid to stand for what's right. But don't wait to address all of these, and then have to correct confusing theology or cultural craziness. Step in and talk to your kids about all the things . . . before they become things! Ask them questions and listen to their answers. Then together search Scripture for God's heart on any topic that comes up. Set the first tracks now, and then watch your kids soar down the hill, secure and free to live in the truth and navigate life well.

A Word to Dads

Well, guys, this chapter covers a lot of important things, and it's definitely not just for the moms.

As a dad, you need to be available and speak to your kids' needs too. They will remember you had important things to say, so use your words well. Most importantly, be sure to weigh your words against God's Word. They need to see how you filter all things through his truth.

Some topics aren't easy. I can slip into my doctor-version of things, approaching the topic of sex like reading from a biology textbook. But my wife is pretty gifted at going straight into the awkward without much hesitation. She picks up the slack for me sometimes. (If your wife is good at that, be glad. But don't shrink back from stepping into the conversations as well.) As a dad, I know I need and want to be available to discuss personal topics like sexuality, gender issues, fears, and doubts—or any other topic where there's confusion or uncertainty. Our boys need to hear a perspective from both Mom and Dad. So it's worth it to push through being a little awkward. You just have to jump in!

Over the past few years, our family has had solid discussions on everything from gender issues to abortion, race, and more. These conversations can be hard, but I have grown from having these talks with my sons, who often offer great perspectives on the topics. I know that because of our good talks, they will be likely to reach out to me as they wrestle with other topics in the future. Your kids have questions on this stuff, so take the lead and be the first to open up the conversation that's waiting to happen.

Dads: Ultimately, your young kids will grow up to be big people, just like you. Though our most hands-on work occurs in those growing-up years, the good news is we have the rest of our lives to know our kids as people. *And hopefully as friends.*

I don't know a better way to wrap up my messages than to remind you of the importance of your role. You'll never get things perfect in parenting (I know I don't!), but your presence, your love, and your commitment are powerful forces in your kids' lives. Step up, lean in, listen, discipline, and love them. They need you, and you'll never regret a moment dedicated to being a great dad.

Monica has some final words to say, but as I close, please know that Monica and I are praying for you and are proud of you.

Now go get busy raising some amazing kids. You've got this!

Thoughts from Josiah, Age Twenty-Two

Parents have the chance to lay "first tracks" in a multitude of ways. My dad really likes Proverbs. I mean, he's probably got half the book memorized by now without even trying. When I was pretty young, he would play an audio recording of Proverbs in the car. I remember hearing Proverbs 9:10, "The fear of the LORD is the beginning of wisdom," on our way to go surfing. I realize now that he was being strategic. He could have listened to anything, but he chose to play Proverbs so that before I even knew what the latest popular radio song was, I heard God's Word.

Though it's not possible to anticipate everything a growing child will face, my parents tried to stay tuned into what we were facing and what was happening in the culture. They brought up subjects over dinner, and often Dad would open the Bible to point us to what God had to say about the topic. Then we'd talk about it. He wasn't preachy, but he made it clear that the only reliable authority was God through his Word.

This process of approaching issues through the lens of Scripture laid first tracks that I still walk in today as I near independence as a young man.

Reflection Questions

1. For what topics have you already "set the first tracks" with your kids?

2. For what topics do you still need to open up conversations?

3. What is a topic with truth that's important to you to impress on your child(ren), and how do you plan to do that?

CHAPTER 15

WHERE AMAZING BEGINS AND ENDS

A Final Note from Monica

And they were all amazed at the greatness of God.
—Luke 9:43

Iwrote the final chapter of my previous book, *Boy Mom*, while flying home from dropping off my firstborn son at college. If you've read it, you might remember how, as I sat through his opening convocation, my mind drifted back to memories of a kindergarten program he was once in. Via some tears on the airplane, I wrote about the contrast between my kindergarten son's eyes desperately searching for his mommy in the crowd with my grown-up son's sure and steady, ready-to-face-the-world (or at least a college campus) gaze as he officially started his higher education.

He was spreading his wings, just as we'd raised him to do.

He was ready, and therefore, I was too. Even if my heart hadn't caught up with the idea yet.

Ironically, I now write this final chapter of *Raising Amazing* while on the airplane headed home from that same son's *college graduation*. That means four years have passed. Four years made up of a million memories. Experiences he couldn't have anticipated but will never forget. Josiah had a wonderful college experience, complete with new best friends, challenging classes, homesick moments, spiritual growth, great adventures, a bit of heartbreak, a crazy pandemic, lots of great surfing, and many new responsibilities.

While he was away, becoming more a man every day, Dave and I were back home, continuing the good, hard work of raising our other three sons. Jonah joined his big brother at college two years ago, and then, *just two weeks ago*, Luke graduated from high school.

Three down. And there begins the mentor/coach stage of parenting as our older boys learn to "adult." Still very important, though different.

As we travel home, Dave and I feel that sweet mix of blissful satisfaction—and complete exhaustion. We're gulping water and toweling off after what feels a bit like a great ball game. *But we're not done*. The game's not over.

Our youngest, Levi, is just wrapping up sixth grade, and we realize our game just went into overtime. That means it's time to regroup. So Dave and I are now giving each other high fives and the pep talk telling ourselves we really do have the energy and the wisdom to raise Levi up to be the amazing young man we believe he too can be.

But the truth is we don't have the energy and wisdom. And we know it. Honestly, we never did. From the beginning of our parenting journey, we consistently proved that our own wisdom and reasoning only fell short.

On our own, *we're fresh out of amazing*.

On our own, we're fresh out of amazing.

Only as we've turned to God, depended on his strength, and trusted his ways have we found the energy to parent well and the wisdom to navigate every season. Only as we've pointed our kids to their awesome Father in heaven have we been able to breathe deeply and sleep soundly, knowing that while we don't have what it takes, he does. In the beginning, at halftime, and, yes, even in overtime.

So whatever stage or season of parenting you're in, I hope this one message in this book sticks with you beyond all the others: *God loves your kids!* More than you could ever imagine. He loves them in their snot-nose naughtiness, in their rascally, rowdy mischief. He loves them when they draw you pictures of flowers and give you the warmest snuggles. And he loves them when their hormones get all weird and their moods prove it. He loves them when they get straight As and when they land in the principal's office. He loves them when they do the dishes without being asked and when they totally forget they're on dish duty. He will never, ever quit loving your kids!

But also, God loves you, Mom and Dad. And he chose *you* to be your child's parent. He knew exactly what he was doing. He loves your heart for wanting to raise them well; he sees every effort, and he hears every prayer. He knows how hard parenting is, and that's why he offers to walk with you through every step of the way, when things look great and when they look bleak. He wants to give you wisdom and counsel. He wants to give you strength, and he even wants to give you sleep (Psalm 127:2)!

We're all likely to come across challenging times in our parenting journey, and if at some point you feel like you're losing the battle, take heart. Do not give up hope! Keep asking God for help, and stay in the game. Do what only you can do, and trust God to do what only he can do.

And when things are going well? Be sure to give God glory.

If your kids score the winning goal or get elected class president or walk an old lady across the street or invent something really special, be sure they know that God has given them every gift. If something about your kids is a pleasant surprise or causes the world to wonder? Make sure that wonder points them to the amazing God behind it all.

Now, together, take hold of God's hand, dive into his Word, rest in his Spirit, and discover his amazing plan for you and your whole family.

With so much love,
Monica (and Dave and the boys)

ACKNOWLEDGMENTS

I have to start by thanking God, my Savior, my Redeemer, the Amazing above all amazings. You are the only perfect parent, and your Word is the very best parenting book. I hope anyone who reads this book is led to read yours even more.

Dave, thank you for partnering with me in this book. I'm not sure you actually signed up for it, but you've been such a good sport! I believe your words to dads are the true gold here. Thank you for patiently enduring all my brainstorming sessions during morning runs, through dinner dates, and as you drifted off to sleep at night. Most of all, thank you for being an amazing dad to our boys. They are blessed beyond belief.

Josiah, Jonah, Luke, and Levi, without you this book would not have been written. You are indeed a pleasant surprise—every day! I pinch myself to think that I get to be your mom. Also, thank you for taking the time to write notes for my chapters and for trusting me to tell your stories. Thank you for making me laugh so hard and pray so hard and love so hard that my heart could explode. I'm so glad we get to be friends forever.

To my parents: You are the most amazing parents and grand-parents anyone could ask for. Your support and encouragement mean the world to me, and your dedication to your grandkids is unsurpassed. Thank you for believing in all of us.

To Dave's dad, Lyn, and his late mom, Karin: Thank you for setting the standard that your son rose up to live out. He is one amazing man, and you are to be thanked. What a legacy!

To Carolyn McCready, my editor: I feel like the most blessed author! What a difference you made in this book-writing process. Your kindness and grace just kept coming, and your feedback and wisdom made this book better. I'd love to keep you as my lifelong editor, and I plan to keep you as my lifelong friend.

To the rest of the team at Zondervan: I am so honored to work with you. From day one I knew I was with a top-notch crew, and I've been impressed every step of the way. Thank you for believing in this book's message.

To Gisele McDaniel: You read every chapter before I turned it in to my editor (kind of like when you clean the house before the house cleaner comes!). I love your beautiful South-African accent and your charm almost as much as your honesty and genuine heart. Thick in the middle of raising your own amazing little firecrackers, you took the time to give me such helpful feedback, especially the perspective of the younger Gen moms. You have great style and quick wit. I hope you write your own book one day.

To my agent, Alex Field: Thank you. It's a privilege to work with you.

To my praying friends: Your unseen talks with our heavenly Father on behalf of this book, its readers, and my family and me were heard. Thank you for your sacrifice of time. (Also, please keep praying. I need you guys!)

To my blog and book readers, podcast listeners, and social media friends: Thank you! You guys make me smile every single day. You have cheered me on and made this process the most fun. I hope and pray this book is a massive encouragement to you, and I wish I could hug each of you personally.

RESOURCES

Thanks for joining me on this journey! I'd love to hear how you and your kids are doing. Use hashtag #raisingamazing on social media to share your kids' shining moments of getting along, honoring God, and doing dishes (and other exceptional tasks) with a happy heart. Be sure to follow and tag @monica swanson_ on Instagram, and I will choose a few winners.

Below is a summary of all the resources mentioned. All links and downloads found at: www.monicaswanson.com/amazingresources.

Links:

Monica's website: www.monicaswanson.com
Monica on Instagram: @monicaswanson_
Character Training Course: www.monicaswanson.com
    /character-course
Raising Tech-Smart Kids Mini-Course:
    www.monicaswanson.com/all-things-technology/

Chapter-by-Chapter Bonus Resources:

Chapter 1:   25 Ways to Show Your Kids You Are All-In
Chapter 2:   Family Mission Statement Template

Chapter 3:   Printable of 1 Corinthians 11:1

Chapter 4:   Bonus chapter: "Amazing Armor: Preparing Your
              Kids to Face Spiritual Battles"

              Steps to Lead Your Child into a Relationship
              with God

Chapter 5:   10 Amazing (and Simple!) Date Night Ideas

Chapter 6:   Scripture-based prayer for our kids to be
              surrounded by good influences

Chapter 7:   List of conversation starters for family meals

Chapter 8:   Bonus chapter: "Motivating Change: A Guide
              for Using Consequences and Discipline in
              Parenting"

              100 Things Kids Can Do Indoors without a Screen

Chapter 9:   A list of books and Bible stories to inspire character

Chapter 10:   A link to the Swanson chore system

              Life Skills by Age List

Chapter 11:   Bonus chapter: "Good and Pleasant: A Guide
              for Conflict Resolution and Peacemaking
              between Siblings"

Chapter 12:   Link to *Truth for Youth Podcast*

              Link to Josiah's book, *Sub-marine*

              15 Character-Inspiring Quotes from Great Athletes

Chapter 13:   Technology Contract Template

              List of filters and accountability software

              Video game guidelines

              Raising Tech-Smart Kids Mini-Course

Chapter 14:   A list of my favorite books and curriculums to
              help give your kids a biblical worldview

              20 Conversations to Have with Your Kids before
              They Launch

              List of resources for navigating difficult cultural
              issues

NOTES

‖‖‖‖‖‖‖‖‖‖‖‖‖‖‖‖‖‖‖‖‖‖‖‖‖‖‖‖‖‖‖‖

A Note to Readers

1. The Free Dictionary, s.v. "amazing," accessed August 19, 2022, https://www.thefreedictionary.com/amazing.

Chapter 1: All-In

1. C. S. Lewis, *Mere Christianity* (New York: HarperCollins, 2021), 11.
2. Kari Kampakis, *More Than a Mom: How Prioritizing Your Wellness Helps You (and Your Family) Thrive* (Nashville: Thomas Nelson, 2022), xx.
3. "Does a Laugh Per Day Keep the Doctor Away?" *U.S. Preventive Medicine*, March 13, 2017, https://www.uspm.com/does-a-laugh-per-day-keep-the-doctor-away/.

Chapter 2: Welcome Aboard

1. Steven John, "Chick-Fil-A Is One of the Most Profitable Fast-Food Chains in the US—Here's Why They're So Successful," *Business Insider*, October 13, 2018, https://www.businessinsider.com/why-chick-fil-a-is-successful-2018-9.
2. Brett and Kate McKay, "Fathering with Intentionality: The Importance of Creating a Family Culture," *Art of Manliness*, September 25, 2021, https://www.artofmanliness.com/people/fatherhood/family-culture/.

3. Rodney and Michelle Gage, *Family Shift* (Franklin, TN: Worthy, 2019), 27.

4. Stephen R. Covey, *The 7 Habits of Highly Effective Families* (New York: Golden, 1997), 93.

5. Covey, *The 7 Habits of Highly Effective Families*, 92.

6. James Clear, *Atomic Habits* (New York: Avery, 2018), 38.

Chapter 3: Parentamorphosis

1. "T. Rowe Price's 11th Annual Parents, Kids & Money Survey," T. Rowe Price, March 2019, https://www.slideshare.net /TRowePrice/t-rowe-prices-11th-annual-parents-kids-money -survey.

2. Cameron Huddleston, "How to Teach Your Kids Good Money Habits," *Forbes*, February 18, 2020, https://www.forbes.com /advisor/personal-finance/how-to-teach-your-kids-good -money-habits/.

3. Karen Robock, "Five Money Fears from Childhood—And How to Overcome Them," MoneySense, December 15, 2021, https:// www.moneysense.ca/financial-literacy/five-money-fears-from -childhood-and-how-to-overcome-them/.

4. Melissa Leong in Robock, "Five Money Fears from Childhood."

Chapter 4: The Very Most Important Thing

1. George Barna, *Revolutionary Parenting* (Carol Stream, IL: Tyndale, 2007), xxi.

2. Tony Evans, *Raising Kingdom Kids* (Carol Stream, IL: Tyndale, 2014), 33.

3. Bob Smietana, "Young Bible Readers More Likely to Be Faithful Adults, Study Finds," *Lifeway Newsroom*, October 17, 2017, https:// news.lifeway.com/2017/10/17/young-bible-readers-more-likely -to-be-faithful-adults-study-finds/.

4. Smietana, "Young Bible Readers More Likely to Be Faithful Adults."

Chapter 5: Focus on the Foundation

1. Justin Whitmel Earley, *Habits of the Household* (Grand Rapids: Zondervan, 2021), 143.
2. David C. Ribar, "Children Raised within Marriage Do Better on Average. Why?" *Child & Family Blog*, October 2015, https:// childandfamilyblog.com/children-marriage-do-better-why/.
3. Robert Quillen in *The Westminster Collection of Christian Quotations: Over 6,000 Quotations Arranged by Theme*, comp. Martin H. Manser (Louisville: Westminster John Knox, 2001), 240.

Chapter 6: The Secret Weapon or the Greatest Danger

1. Tony Evans, *Raising Kingdom Kids* (Carol Stream, IL: Tyndale, 2014), 29.
2. "Child Sexual Abuse Facts," YWCA, September 2017, https:// www.ywca.org/wp-content/uploads/WWV-CSA-Fact-Sheet -Final.pdf.
3. Michael Robb, "Tweens, Teens, and Phones: What Our 2019 Research Reveals," *Common Sense*, https://www.commonsensemedia .org/kids-action/articles/tweens-teens-and-phones-what-our-2019 -research-reveals.

Chapter 7: Home Base

1. "Family Meals: More than Good Nutrition," *Stanford Children's Health*, accessed August 19, 2022, https://www.stanfordchildrens .org/en/topic/default?id=family-meals-more-than-good -nutrition-1-2152.
2. Justin Whitmel Earley, *Habits of the Household: Practicing the Story of God in Everyday Family Rhythms* (Grand Rapids: Zondervan, 2021), 4–5.

Chapter 8: Nos and Yeses

1. Dan Mager, "Why Sometimes Saying 'No' to Your Kids Is So Important," *Psychology Today*, January 20, 2019, https://www

.psychologytoday.com/us/blog/some-assembly-required/201901
/why-sometimes-saying-no-your-kids-is-so-important.

2. Mariam Arain et al., "Maturation of the Adolescent Brain,"
National Library of Medicine 9 (April 3, 2013): 449–461, https://
doi.org/10.2147/NDT.S39776.

3. Drew Dyck, *Your Future Self Will Thank You: Secrets to Self-Control
from the Bible and Brain Science* (Chicago: Moody, 2019), 15.

4. Michael Gottfredson, "Self-Control Theory and Crime," *Oxford
Research Encyclopedia of Criminology and Criminal Justice*, July 27,
2017, https://doi.org/10.1093/acrefore/9780190264079.013.252.

5. Robin Berman, *Permission to Parent* (New York: HarperCollins,
2014), 13.

6. George Barna, *Revolutionary Parenting* (Carol Stream, IL: Tyndale,
2007), xxi.

7. Robin Berman, "How to Reverse Negotiate with Your Child," Kids
in the House, December 19, 2014, YouTube video, https://www
.youtube.com/watch?v=aLksOPijy7A&feature=emb_logo.

8. Justin Whitmel Earley, *Habits of the Household* (Grand Rapids:
Zondervan, 2021), 100.

Chapter 9: Dish Duty

1. Michelle Schwantes, "Warren Buffett Thinks You Should Hire for
Integrity First. Here Are 5 Questions to Ask Job Candidates," *Inc.*,
June 29, 2021, https://www.inc.com/marcel-schwantes/warren
-buffett-thinks-you-should-hire-for-integrity-first-here-are-5
-questions-to-ask-job-candidates.html.

Chapter 10: The Struggle Is Real (and Also Good)

1. *Helen Keller's Journal: 1936-1937* (New York: Doubleday, Doran &
Company, Inc., 1938), 60.

2. Jim Haudan, "Adversity Is the Fuel of Greatness," *Inc.*, December
2016, https://www.inc.com/jim-haudan/adversity-is-the-fuel-of
-greatness.html.

3. Haudan, "Adversity Is the Fuel of Greatness."

Chapter 11: Help Siblings Become Friends

1. Robert J. Waldinger, George E. Vaillant, and E. John Orav, "Childhood Sibling Relationships as a Predictor of Major Depression in Adulthood: A 30-Year Prospective Study," *American Journal of Psychiatry* 6, vol. 164 (June 2007): 949–954, https://doi.org/10.1176/ajp.2007.164.6.949.

2. Anna Goldfarb, "How to Maintain Sibling Relationships," *New York Times*, May 8, 2018, https://www.nytimes.com/2018/05/08/smarter-living/how-to-maintain-sibling-relationships.html.

3. Lisa Kadane, "Will Your Kids Be Friends as Adults?" *Today's Parent*, June 29, 2020, https://www.todaysparent.com/family/family-life/will-your-kids-be-friends-as-adults/.

Chapter 12: How They Spend Their Days

1. Casey Eggleston and Jason Fields, "Census Bureau's Household Pulse Survey Shows Significant Increase in Homeschooling Rates in Fall 2020," United States Census Bureau, March 22, 2021, https://www.census.gov/library/stories/2021/03/homeschooling-on-the-rise-during-covid-19-pandemic.html.

2. Amy Norton, "Physically Active Teens Stay out of Trouble," NBCNewYork, August 28, 2008, https://www.nbcnewyork.com/news/health/physically_active_teens_stay_out_of_trouble/2113620/.

3. Paul S. Carbone et al., "Promoting the Participation of Children and Adolescents with Disabilities in Sports, Recreation, and Physical Activity," *Pediatrics* 6, vol. 148 (December 2021): e2021054664, https://doi.org/10.1542/peds.2021-054664.

Chapter 13: All the Screens!

1. "Pornography Statistics," CovenantEyes, accessed August 19, 2022, https://www.covenanteyes.com/pornstats/.

2. Jonathan McKee, *Parenting Generation Screen* (Carol Stream, IL: Tyndale, 2021), 52.

3. McKee, *Parenting Generation Screen*, 52.

4. "Screen Time and Children," American Academy of Child & Adolescent Psychiatry, updated February 2022, https://www .aacap.org/AACAP/Families_and_Youth/Facts_for_Families /FFF-Guide/Children-And-Watching-TV-054.

5. "Family Media Plan," The American Academy of Pediatrics, accessed August 19, 2022, https://www.healthychildren.org /English/media/Pages/default.aspx.

6. Chris Matyszczyk, "Bill Gates: My Kids Didn't Have Cell Phones Until They Were 14," *CNET*, April 21, 2017, https://www.cnet .com/culture/bill-gates-my-kids-didnt-have-cell-phones-till -they-were-14/.

7. Steven Reinberg, "Here's How Too Much Social Media Can Harm Girls," WebMD, August 14, 2019, https://www.webmd.com /mental-health/news/20190814/heres-how-too-much-social -media-can-harm-girls.

8. Monica Swanson, Raising Tech-Smart Kids Mini-Course, https:// courses.monicaswanson.com.

Chapter 14: First Tracks

1. Kari Kampakis, "Setting the First Tracks: How to Have Hard Conversations with Your Kids," February 7, 2016, https://www .karikampakis.com/2016/02/setting-the-first-tracks-how-to -have-hard-conversations-with-your-kids/.

2. Kampakis, "Setting the First Tracks."

3. Jonathan "JP" Pokluda, *Outdated: Find Love That Lasts When Dating Has Changed* (Grand Rapids: Baker, 2021), 14–15.

4. Pokluda, *Outdated*, 22.

From the Publisher

GREAT BOOKS

ARE EVEN BETTER WHEN THEY'RE SHARED!

Help other readers find this one:

- Post a review at your favorite online bookseller

- Post a picture on a social media account and share why you enjoyed it

- Send a note to a friend who would also love it—or better yet, give them a copy

Thanks for reading!